This book is writt

- set but don't complete important goals
- make and break New Year's resolutions in the same month
- have unfulfilled dreams and need help achieving them
- want a daily source of inspiration
- love powerful, motivational quotes
- sometimes want a refreshing mental lift during the day
- need a perfect gift for any occasion

This book is also written for...

- **executives** looking for a way to recognize valued employees
- **managers** helping employees set and achieve goals
- **parents** guiding their children to learn goal setting
- **teachers** wanting to start their classes with a motivating quote
- **sales people** recharging their energy all day long
- **trainers** searching for inspiring quotes to power up their presentations
- **high school and college graduates** starting to define their paths to success
- **job seekers** pursuing new career opportunities
- **individuals and groups** working through recovery programs
- **change agents** building commitment around new team objectives
- **network marketers** encouraging others to fulfill their dreams
- **anyone** embarking on a path of self-improvement

To Julie and Rick,

Thanks for all your valued support and encouragement when I was just getting my business started. You are good friends. Jerry

Instant Inspiration

Using Quotes
to Guide You to
Your Goals

by Jerry Jerome

Instant Inspiration
Using Quotes to Guide You to Your Goals
by Jerry Jerome

Published and Distributed by:
Instant Wisdom Publishing
Post Office Box 93006
Phoenix, AZ 85070-3006 U.S.A.
(480) 759-2987
(877) 791-2987

www.instantwisdompublishing.com

ISBN: 0-9726169-0-X
Library of Congress Control Number: 2003100430

Editing and Project Management: Karla Olson, Via Press, Phoenix, Arizona
Interior Design: Lisa Liddy, The Printed Page, Phoenix, Arizona
Cover Design: Robert Howard Graphic Design, Fort Collins, Colorado

Printed in the United States of America

First Printing: July, 2003
9 8 7 6 5 4 3 2 1

Dedication

This book is lovingly dedicated
in memory of my parents,

Eve Jerome
and
Jerry Jerome

who enriched me with their love
and inspired me with their lives

Instant Inspiration

Contents

Acknowledgments

I use not only all the brains I have,
but all I can borrow.
Woodrow Wilson

My deepest love and gratitude go to my wife, Kathy, for believing in me and encouraging me to follow my dreams; and for tirelessly reviewing every sentence, quote and exercise (many times) to help make this book the best it could be.

A million hugs, kisses and thanks to my daughter, Samantha, and son, Jake, for being so patient and loving (for *so* long) while I plugged away on this book.

Many thanks to my brothers: Al, Bill, and Jim, who inspire me with their talents and challenge me to develop my own.

My sincerest appreciation to the entire Jerome, Frankel, and Dietz families, especially Elaine Jerome, and Gerri and Norman Dietz, whose unconditional love and steadfast support have meant so much to me.

A special thank you to Sharon and Michael Palestine for their lifelong friendship and loving hearts.

Many thanks to special friends who have contributed so much to my life in so many ways: Kevin Foley, Diane Goff, Michelle Hernandez, Mitzi Jobes, Renee LaCour, Bob Mosby, and Greg Zobell.

Thank you to Karla Olson, my editor, for her guidance and many contributions to this book.

I want to acknowledge all the inspirational giants who are quoted throughout this book, and especially a few key sources of wisdom whose words (and lives) have made a significant impact on my life: Stephen R. Covey, Napoleon Hill, Richard J. Leider, Maxwell Maltz, Earl Nightingale, Ram Dass, Brian Tracy, and Zig Ziglar.

Last, but certainly most, I want to thank God for inspiring me throughout this project. "May the words of my mouth and the meditation of my heart be pleasing in your sight, O Lord, my Rock and my Redeemer." (Psalm 19:14)

Part One

Celebrating Success

Cultivating Dreams

Evaluating Efforts

Setting Goals

Developing Perseverance

Making Plans

Reinforcing Accomplishments

Aligning Attitude

Overcoming Obstacles

Disciplining Action

Introduction

Welcome to a very different kind of book on goal achievement.

Though you can read *Instant Inspiration* in an hour you will use it for a lifetime. You can read the quotes again and again, not only as a guide to achieving lifetime goals, but to help start your day in the right frame of mind, give you a head-clearing, mid-day mental lift, provide instant inspiration before an important meeting, or even to counteract the negative influence of difficult people. You'll begin to think of it as your partner in success.

On Your Mark, Get Set, Goal!

Goals are declarations about your dreams and desires. They identify what you really value and want in your life. Setting goals is a powerful tool for self-realization because it converts dreams into goals, goals into plans, plans into actions, and actions into results. But goal setting is not something that you do once and then forget. It is a discipline, a way of thinking that shows you value your time, your energy, and your life. And you must constantly work at it to achieve lifelong success.

Why I Wrote this Book

Plato wrote, "The true creator is necessity, who is the mother of invention." This was true in my case; I wrote this book because I needed it.

Have you ever made New Year's resolutions, only to abandon them soon after? I have. Have you ever written the same resolutions several years in a row without following through? Me, too. Have you ever set an important goal that was in your best interest, such as losing weight, managing stress, getting organized, or starting an exercise program, but couldn't seem to make it happen? We all have.

Many people I coach experience the same frustration trying to keep their personal and professional goals and resolutions on the front burner, only to see them pushed aside by more urgent, but less important, demands. This is normal and not the result of some character flaw or personality defect. It usually comes from a failure to understand the process by which we establish and achieve goals. This book outlines the principles and practices that ensure that you achieve the goals you set.

Why Quotes?

For most of my adult life and in my work as a therapist, consultant, coach, writer, and educator I've collected and used quotes. At the end of my presentations, people often ask for copies of the quotes I used because they found them motivating and helpful in remembering the points of the workshop, but also because they wanted to share the quotes with colleagues, friends, and family members.

One of the reasons people love quotes so much is that they convey, in a few well chosen words, a great truth. So much wisdom in such a small package inspires us to hold onto it and learn from it. Quotes are neat little bundles of inspiration that help us see things more clearly.

If you look through the index, you will see a broad spectrum of famous people, ancient to modern, representing many fields of expertise. These people have come up with such memorable sayings because they have the ability and insight to distill the essence of their experiences into eloquent words. Many of them are great speakers and writers, and have a fluency with language that helps them express profound thoughts in very memorable words. These great ideas are there to coach us as much as to enlighten us. Think of the authors of these quotes as your teachers of success.

When I came up with the idea for this book, I sifted through my quote collection looking for thoughts on goal achievement. In order to make these quotes useful, I organized them around key phases in the goal achieving process. Each quote has been carefully selected and sequenced to communicate a powerful point about that phase. Sometimes I deliberately included several quotes that make a similar statement because of the importance of the message or because I know that different people will respond to different quotes.

The Benefits of Having Goals

Imagine you are going on a trip. You get in the car and start driving, then after several hours, you realize you don't know where you're going or where you are, and you discover you don't have a map. What would you do? Would you keep driving, or stop and buy a map? Unfortunately, too many people keep driving, just as too many people fail to reach a desirable destination because they don't plan their journey.

In this example, the trip is your life, the destination stands for your goals, and the map is the plans you follow to get there. There is a saying that goes, "If you don't know where you're going, any road will take you there." It's very unlikely you will get anywhere you want to go without goals and plans to guide you. It's no coincidence that goals have been referred to as the road map to success, yet it's estimated that fewer than 5 percent of the population sets and achieves them.

People will give lots of reasons why they fail to set goals. Some say they are afraid to fail, while others claim they don't know how to create them. The most common reason people offer is that they simply don't have the time. In reality, the number one reason people don't set and achieve goals is that they don't take the time to decide exactly what it is they want in life and then figure out how to get it.

There are many excellent reasons why making the time to go through the goal-setting process may be one of the most important activities you ever do. Setting and achieving goals will help you:

- discover who you are by learning what's important to you

- create a sense of purpose for your life

- provide direction and focused action toward objectives

- achieve more, in less time, with improved efficiency

- break through procrastination and build effectiveness

- increase your self-confidence and self-esteem

- experience pride in your work and satisfaction in your life

- boost your motivation when you overcome difficult challenges

- focus more on what's important rather than just what's urgent

- have peace of mind and decrease stress, anxiety, and worry

- develop balance between the important areas of your life

- learn how to get from where you are to where you want to be

If you're ready to achieve your goals and inspire yourself to success, turn the page and let's begin.

Instant Inspiration

How to Get the Most from this Book

What do you want from this book? There are several ways to approach its wisdom. If you'd like a daily dose of inspiration, open it anywhere and dive in. You'll find insight on every page. If you prefer a methodical way to turn your dreams into reality, glance through the action plan (see p.169) and follow a step-by-step path to success.

Sharing this book's wisdom with others will increase your own understanding of it. Articulating what you've learned to others deepens your command of the goal achievement process, sustains your motivation, and provides invaluable support along the path to success.

Here are some additional ideas for getting the most from this book:

Families   Families who work through the book together can support one another as they progress. Discussing favorite quotes and posting them on the refrigerator, bathroom mirror or dinner table helps build a positive atmosphere and reinforces the message of success.

Coaches and Counselors   Coaches and counselors can be invaluable partners in accomplishing your goals by providing guidance, encouragement, motivation, perspective, and problem-solving help. Their ongoing support can

	strengthen your resolve to honor your commitments.
Support Groups	Regular meetings with supportive friends provide a safe environment for sharing dreams and setting personal goals, reporting on progress and receiving feedback, getting help with problems and sustaining motivation, and evaluating efforts and celebrating success.
Teams	Work teams and department staff can achieve group goals by working through the steps while developing team cohesiveness. The team approach opens up communication, improves human relations skills, builds trust, resolves conflicts, and enhances commitment, both among team members and to the organization.

A Plan for Reading this Book

This book consists of two major sections designed to be used either independently or interdependently. You can read the quotes apart from the action plan, or you can use the quotes and action plan together.

If you are more interested in the quotes, remember that they have been selected and positioned so that when you read them together, they speak with one voice—that of an inspirational coach helping you understand a phase in the goal achievement process. Read the quotes in sequence to get the overall message of each chapter, then focus on individual quotes that resonate for you.

If you choose to use the quotes and action plan together, after reading the quotes in each phase, complete the exercises in the appropriate step of the action plan.

Methodically proceeding through the book in this fashion allows you to accomplish three things:

1. Inspire yourself to success using these words of wisdom

2. Learn the tools and techniques for achieving any goal you strongly desire

3. Work on accomplishing your goals

By the time you reach the end of the book, you could complete one or more small goals.

A Way to Read Quotes

Reading a quote book is different than reading other kinds of books. You could sit down and plow through this book cover-to-cover, but to really reap its benefits, take time to savor the words you read. There's no value in rushing through this book. If you do, you'll miss most of what's in it. Stop and pay attention to the words and names of the many famous people who speak to you throughout this book. React to the quotes as you read, then dig deeply for the value and unique meaning for you. Most importantly, think how you can apply the wisdom of these quotes to your goals and your life.

When you read quotes, you are not reading for information, but for inspiration. Let them take you to another level of consciousness, center you, motivate you, energize you, and remind you of what you already know to be true but may have forgotten.

Something strange and wonderful happens when you read a quote that resonates deeply within you. You might feel an energy surge in your chest, or give an affirmative nod as you read. You might even mutter "Yes" out loud. It stimulates and quickens your physical, mental, and emotional centers and motivates you to take action on what you read. This resonance is one of the primary goals of this book. Pay attention to it as you read.

My hope for you is that this book becomes a guide and a source of renewal that you return to often; a resource that can help clarify your path to achievement.

A Note about Attribution

I have done my best to accurately attribute the quotes. Some have been passed down and cannot be traced to an exact source. If you find that I have inaccurately attributed any quote, please send me a correction and a source for that quote and I will change it in the next edition of the book.

The Master Strategies of Goal Setting

There are a number of established goal-setting principles and strategies that dramatically increase your likelihood of success. Because there's nearly universal agreement about their importance, I call them "The Master Strategies of Goal Setting."

Read these strategies and become acquainted with the essentials of good goal setting. More importantly, review them later, while you work on your action plan. The more you apply these principles, the greater your odds of success, not only with achieving goals but with life in general.

1. **Write down your goals.**
   Until you write down your goals they are merely wishes. Your written goals become your road map to success. This single action helps in multiple ways. Writing your goals solidifies your commitment to them and stimulates your desire to reach them. It makes your goals real and gives you a sense of urgency. You will have a record of your progress and success will be easier to measure.

2. **Focus precedes success.**
   You can do anything you want in life, but you can't do everything at once. It's great to have multiple goals, but counterproductive to work on too many at one time. Saying "yes" to one thing means saying "no" to another. If you have too many

commitments, it's easy to lose focus in the crush of daily pressures and interruptions. Those who succeed are those who stay focused on the really important things. It's best to fix on just a few manageable goals to begin with. Spreading yourself too thin dilutes focus and weakens efforts, which could cause you to abandon your goals entirely.

3. **Set performance goals over outcome goals.**
   Performance goals are based upon actions you take and are under your control. Outcome goals are dependent upon other people's behavior and are, therefore, more difficult to predict. An example of a performance goal might be to make 20 percent more sales calls this year than last year. Your success depends solely on behavior that you take. You are competing only with yourself and your past performance. A related outcome goal might be to be the top salesperson in your company. There are many uncontrollable variables that could prevent you from achieving this goal, regardless of your behavior. Incidentally, in this example, achieving the performance goal just might get you the outcome goal as well.

4. **Always keep your goals in front of you.**
   Sustaining motivation and momentum is one of the biggest challenges in achieving your goals. Urgent issues that occur in daily life make it easy to lose sight of goals and lose momentum. Make sure you don't forget your goals. Place visual reminders around your home and office. Start each day by reviewing your goals, plans, and daily action steps. Finish each day by reviewing and

evaluating your progress. Perhaps write a journal entry about what you accomplished that day and what you plan to do tomorrow.

5. **Surround yourself with a network of supportive and successful people.**
Successful people know they never succeed on their own; they're aware of the critical need for support players. Share your goals with trusted family and friends who are positive and encouraging. Study the successful people in your field and identify what you can learn from them. Ask them for help and you'll be amazed at how willing they are to share their expertise with you. Just as important, help others along the way when they ask for it.

6. **Create goals that you are passionate about.**
People with passion have the power to make things happen, get results, and make a difference. To cultivate passion, focus on goals that are meaningful to you, utilize your strengths and interests, and contribute to yourself and others in a significant way. Your success will fuel your passion for achieving bigger and better goals in the future.

7. **Aim tall but think small.**
Thinking small doesn't mean lacking ambition; it means taking your big, ambitious goals and breaking them down into sub-goals and action steps small enough to accomplish. Goals are statements of intention, not action, and are not achievable until you reduce them to actions that can be completed. Ultimate success is built on a long string of small successes that happen every day of your life.

8. **If you want different results, do different things.**
Many say they want to achieve their goals, but fail to do what's necessary to attain success. Either they're unaware of how to proceed, or they have a long list of excuses that prevent progress. If you're not satisfied with what you've accomplished, you need to change how you think about goals, how you set and go about achieving your goals, and how you think about yourself in relation to having what you want. The quotes and exercises in this book will direct you to do the things that will get you the results you desire.

9. **Remain flexible.**
It's a big mistake to think of goals as being etched in granite. They're but a blueprint for success. Goals have to flex to reflect reality as people and circumstances change. In order to keep goals relevant, they must be reviewed constantly and revised as needed. Be willing to adjust both methods and time frames to accommodate life's changes.

10. **Success is a journey, not a destination.**
Focus on where you want to go, how and when you want to get there, and especially, how to make the trip a wonderful learning experience. Balance concern about reaching your destination with concern for the quality of the journey. Your trip must be traveled one day at a time, so fill each day with enjoyment, excellence, and love.

Part Two

Celebrating
Success

Cultivating
Dreams

Evaluating
Efforts

Setting
Goals

Developing
Perseverance

Making
Plans

Reinforcing
Accomplishments

Aligning
Attitude

Overcoming
Obstacles

Disciplining
Action

Achieving Your Goals in Ten Phases

You can turn your dreams into reality by achieving your goals if you apply a rational, phase-by-phase process. Each phase increases your personal power as it shortens the distance between you and your ambitions. By following each phase and completing the action plan included in this book, you'll master the tools that will enable you to realize any future you desire.

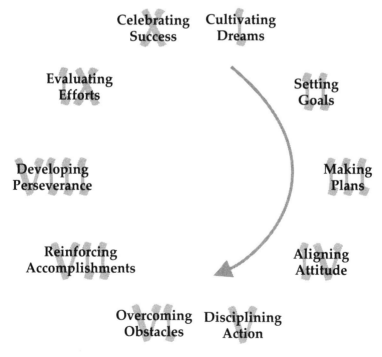

Achieving Your Goals in Ten Phases

Phase One: Cultivating Dreams

Identify the important things you want to be, do, see, have, and experience that can give your life its greatest meaning, challenge, and satisfaction. This phase can reveal your life's passion and purpose so you can make some decisions about what achievements would give you the most joy and fulfillment.

Phase Two: Setting Goals

Setting goals is one of the most important things you will ever do to achieve success. Goals have been called "dreams with a deadline." In this phase you convert your dreams into Specific, Measurable, Achievable, Relevant, and Timed objectives that instantly move you in the direction of your desired result.

Phase Three: Making Plans

If goals are the road map to success, then making effective plans is the secret to achieving your goals. In this phase you turn your goal statements into operational plans—down to tasks that you can schedule on a weekly and daily planner. The only way to achieve your goals is step-by-step.

Phase Four: Aligning Attitude

Without the right attitude, striving for goals can degenerate into drudgery, just another entry on your endless "to-do" list. Enthusiasm is the attitude that achieves goals. By infusing your goals with enthusiasm, you mobilize your actions with spirit and vitality. This cements your commitment to the things you dearly want.

Phase Five: Disciplining Action

Success requires disciplined action. Focus on the small positive progress you make every day, and don't get discouraged about what you don't accomplish. The essence of this phase is forming habits that reinforce your commitment to your goals. Remember, it isn't how fast you're going that is important, but what direction you're headed.

Phase Six: Overcoming Obstacles

Most goal-related obstacles are inevitable by-products of growth and change, and they accompany the pursuit of all important goals. They highlight when there's a need for new knowledge, skills, or perspective. To manage them you must adopt a creative, problem-solving approach.

Phase Seven: Reinforcing Accomplishments

Basic psychology tells us behavior that is reinforced tends to be repeated. It's important to reinforce all positive steps and accomplishments so you repeat them again and again. Planned reinforcements along the journey to your goals make the trip much more rewarding. Plan your "treats" to make each milestone motivating.

Phase Eight: Developing Perseverance

Goal-setting success comes down to perseverance, which is the heart and soul of achievement. It takes commitment and focus to keep goals alive and to keep moving toward them. Developing perseverance is about character. You have to eliminate the word "quit" from your vocabulary if you want to achieve your goals.

Phase Nine: Evaluating Efforts

This phase is about exploring where you are, what you've learned, and what you need to do to complete your goals. It's important to learn everything you can from your experiences so that you can build habits of effectiveness that can help you achieve any goal you desire.

Phase Ten: Celebrating Success

It's time to reward yourself for a job well done. Make your celebration proportional to your achievement. Don't forget to make a record of all your goal successes. Finish this process by setting new goals that are more challenging, more interesting, and more motivating. You did it once, you can do it again—only better.

The sequence of these phases isn't set in stone. Often you'll find yourself working on several phases simultaneously, even sometimes out of sequence. It is important that you address each phase, however, and once you're familiar with them, experiment to find the most efficient and effective way to make them work for you.

Phase One

X Cultivating Dreams

IX

VIII

VII

VI V

IV

III

II

Cultivating Dreams

The first phase to achieving goals is to realize you have some. To learn what your goals are, you have to cultivate your dreams. This involves identifying those known and hidden aspirations that can give your life its greatest meaning, challenge, and satisfaction. Cultivating your dreams can reveal your life's passion and purpose so you can make some decisions about what achievements would give you the most joy and fulfillment.

It's unfortunate that many people associate dreams with unrealistic expectations. In truth, dreams can be the visions that inspire our greatest accomplishments. All great accomplishments started out as someone's dream. Dreams have the power to produce miraculous things. But, for most people, their dreams remain just dreams, either because they don't believe they can achieve them or they don't know how. This book will show you ways to remedy both.

In this important first phase, you need to suspend your judgment about what's realistic and push your imagination to identify as many dreams as you can, in as many areas of life as you can think of. Don't worry about how you're going to achieve your dreams at this stage. That will come in the next several phases. For now, you're just trying to capture dreams, both big and small, that float around in your head.

Make sure to stretch your mind to come up with your big dreams as well as your more easily attainable dreams. Big dreams can create a success momentum of their own and can inspire extraordinary effort toward their achievement.

Finally, make sure your dreams are YOUR dreams and not someone else's dreams for you. You'll know if they're your dreams by how you feel when you think about them. If they leave you flat, forget about them. They're probably someone else's dreams for you. If they sound reasonable, they're worth writing down. If they quicken your pulse, you're onto something important. If just thinking about them inspires your soul, consider yourself among the most fortunate; you've been given a very special gift.

The quotes in this phase explore:

- All great achievements start as someone's dream.

- Your work in life is to discover your dreams and make them come true.

- One great dream can change your life.

Cultivating Dreams

Nothing happens unless first a dream.
Carl Sandburg

If you can dream it, you can do it.
Walt Disney

Everything starts as somebody's dream.
Larry Niven

All men who have achieved great things
have been dreamers.
Orison Swett Marden

What the mind can conceive and believe,
it can achieve.
Napoleon Hill

We are what we pretend to be,
so we must be careful
about what we pretend to be.
Kurt Vonnegut

We are what we think.
All that we are arises with our thoughts.
With our thoughts we create the world.
Buddha

What would you attempt to do
if you knew you could not fail?
Robert Schuller

We all have possibilities we don't know about.
We can do things we don't even dream we can do.
Dale Carnegie

The future fairly startles me
with its impending greatness.
We are on the verge of undreamed progress.
Henry Ford

Cherish your visions and your dreams
as they are the children of your soul;
the blueprint of your ultimate achievements.
Napoleon Hill

Man is so made that whenever anything
fires his soul, impossibilities vanish.
Jean de la Fontaine

There is nothing like a dream to create the future.
Utopia today, flesh and blood tomorrow.
Victor Hugo

You are today where your thoughts brought you;
you will be tomorrow where your thoughts take you.
James Allen

There is no security in this life.
There is only opportunity.
Douglas MacArthur

We are confronted
with insurmountable opportunities.
Walt Kelly

To improve the golden moment of opportunity
and catch the good that is within our reach,
is the great art of life.
Samuel Johnson

What you can do is limited
only by what you can dream.
Dick Rutan

Only he who can see the invisible
can do the impossible.
Frank Gaines

In dreams begin our possibilities.
William Shakespeare

Imagination is more important than knowledge.
Albert Einstein

Man, alone, has the power to transform
his thoughts into physical reality;
man, alone, can dream
and make his dreams come true.
Napoleon Hill

Life is the business of making
desires and dreams come true.
Jack Grossman

The future belongs to those who believe
in the beauty of their dreams.
Eleanor Roosevelt

Go confidently in the direction of your dreams
and act as though it were impossible to fail.
Dorothea Brande

Dreams are the touchstones of our characters.
Henry David Thoreau

It is never too late to be
what you might have been.
George Eliot

To make a great dream come true,
you must first have a great dream.
Hans Selye

Dream big dreams,
only big dreams have the power
to move men's souls.
Marcus Aurelius

You have to think big to be big.
Claude M. Bristol

Shoot for the moon.
Even if you miss it you will land among the stars.
Les Brown

Just one great idea can completely
revolutionize your life.
Earl Nightingale

Dream lofty dreams, and as you dream,
so shall you become.
Your vision is the promise
of what you shall one day be;
your ideal is the prophecy
of what you shall at last unveil.
James Allen

What lies behind us and what lies before us
are tiny matters compared to what lies within us.
Ralph Waldo Emerson

Our truest life is when we are in our dreams awake.
Henry David Thoreau

All our dreams can come true—
if we have the courage to pursue them.
Walt Disney

It takes a lot of courage
to show your dreams to someone else.
Erma Bombeck

Every really new idea looks crazy at first.
Abraham H. Maslow

The person with a new idea is a crank
until the idea succeeds.
Mark Twain

Some men see things as they are and say, "Why?"
I dream things that never were,
and say, "Why not?"
George Bernard Shaw

To give life meaning
one must have a purpose
larger than one's self.
Will Durant

The purpose of life after all is to live it,
to taste the experience to the utmost,
to reach out eagerly and without fear
for newer and richer experiences.
Eleanor Roosevelt

Nobody succeeds beyond
his or her wildest expectations
unless he or she begins
with some wild expectations.
Ralph Charrell

Life is largely a matter of expectation.
Horace

To understand the heart and mind of a person,
look not at what he has already achieved,
but at what he aspires to do.
Kahlil Gibran

Let yourself be silently drawn
by the strange pull of what you really love.
It will not lead you astray.
Rumi

Discovery consists of seeing
what everybody has seen
and thinking what nobody has thought.
Albert Szent-Gyorgi

Imagination is the beginning of creation.
You imagine what you desire,
you will what you imagine,
and at last you create what you will.
George Bernard Shaw

A man to carry on a successful business
must have imagination.
He must see things as in a vision,
a dream of the whole thing.
Charles M. Schwab

Dreams pass into the reality of action.
From the action stems the dreams again;
and this interdependence produces
the highest form of living.
Anaïs Nin

I dream my painting
and then I paint my dream.
Vincent Van Gogh

31

Vision is the art
of seeing things invisible.
Jonathan Swift

Imagination is everything.
Carl Jung

Your imagination is your preview
of life's coming attractions.
Albert Einstein

Genius means little more than the faculty
of perceiving in an unhabitual way.
William James

What we need is more people
who specialize in the impossible.
Theodore Roethke

If you do not express your own original ideas,
if you do not listen to your own being,
you will have betrayed yourself.
Rollo May

Don't part with your illusions.
When they are gone, you may still exist,
but you have ceased to live.
Mark Twain

Don't be afraid your life will end;
be afraid that it will never begin.
Grace Hansen

We grow through our dreams.
All great men and women are dreamers.
Some, however, allow their dreams to die.
You should nurse your dreams and protect them
through bad times and tough times
to the sunshine and light which always comes.
Woodrow Wilson

It is the first of all problems for a man
to find out what kind of work
he is to do in this universe.
Thomas Carlyle

No man is born into the world
whose work is not born with him.
James Russell Lowell

Your work is to discover your work
and then with all your heart
to give yourself to it.
Buddha

A man's main task in life
is to give birth to himself.
Erich Fromm

Each man has his own vocation.
The talent is the call.
There is one direction in which
all space is open to him.
Ralph Waldo Emerson

Each man must look to himself
to teach him the meaning of life.
It is not something discovered;
it is something moulded.
Antoine de Saint-Exupery

For a man to achieve
all that is demanded of him
he must regard himself
as greater than he is.
Johann Wolfgang von Goethe

Everyone has a potential,
in essence, built into them.
And if we are to live life to the fullest,
we must realize that potential.
Norman Vincent Peale

Every person is born to be a star at something.
The purpose of his life is to discover it
and then spend his years building upon
that plot of ground it was given him to till.
Earl Nightingale

Every man is the architect of his own fortune.
Sallust

So, in the jungle of our fantasy,
you might decide to search for some ultimate goal,
some heroic mission there,
that would be a burning driving force in your life.
Richard Nelson Bolles

If one advances confidently
in the direction of his dreams,
and endeavors to live the life which he has imagined,
he will meet with a success
unexpected in common hours.
Henry David Thoreau

At that point in your life
where your talent meets the needs of the world,
that is where God wants you to be.
Albert Schweitzer

To every man there comes in his lifetime
that special moment when he is figuratively tapped
on the shoulder and offered the chance
to do a very special thing,
unique to him and fitted to his talent;
what a tragedy if that moment
finds him unprepared or unqualified
for the work which would be his finest hour.
Winston Churchill

No matter how qualified and deserving we are,
we will never reach a better life
until we can imagine it for ourselves
and allow ourselves to have it.
Richard Bach

Miracles occur in direct proportion
to your willingness to have them.
Werner Erhard

It's always fun to do the impossible.
Walt Disney

The only way to discover the limits of the possible
is to go beyond them into the impossible.
Arthur C. Clarke

We cannot become what we need to be
by remaining what we are.
Max DePree

Let us become the change we seek in this world.
Mohandas K. Gandhi

The best way to make your dreams come true
is to wake up.
Paul Valery

Somebody should tell us,
right at the start of our lives,
that we are dying.
Then we might live to the limit,
every minute of every day.
Do it, I say.
Whatever you want to do, do it now.
There are only so many tomorrows.
Michael Landon

Phase Two

Setting Goals

Goals have been called dreams with a deadline. When dreams remain vague and abstract, they can't be worked on or achieved. Happiness, wealth, or peace of mind are too general to be called goals. But when you take those dreams and convert them into statements that are easy to understand, communicate, measure, implement, and evaluate then you make them goals that motivate you to action. You transform them into powerful statements that instantly move you in the direction of your desired results.

These are called S.M.A.R.T. goals. The S.M.A.R.T. acronym is a widely recognized formula in goal setting that is helpful in converting vague dreams and wishes into focused, targeted commitments that facilitate achievement.

Let's define each of the characteristics:

Specific: Describe your goal in a clear, detailed, and focused way so that you know exactly what you want to accomplish and what will be different once your goal is achieved. Remember that a goal is a statement of an end result, not the activities needed to achieve that result. Also, it's more motivating to state your goal as a positive achievement rather than a negative one. For instance, say "I will weigh ___ pounds by June 1st" rather than "I will lose 20 pounds by June 1st."

Measurable: Describe your goal in terms that can be objectively measured and evaluated. This is easiest when you add a quantitative criteria for measuring progress and completion of the goal. The above example contains the necessary measure that will make it easy to determine success.

Achievable: Does your goal seem realistically attainable? The level of difficulty in achieving your goal determines your motivation. If you perceive your goal as either too easy or too hard, you will be less motivated. Goals need to be challenging enough to test your skills and abilities, but not so difficult that you get discouraged and give up or give less than your best effort.

Relevant: Is this truly your own or is this a goal others want you to achieve? People often abandon goals pushed on them by others because the payoff isn't worth the price. If your goals are important to you, they're relevant goals. Your goals should contribute to the kind of life you want to create.

Timely: Establish a target date for your goal and also dates for the completion of milestones or sub-goals. Such dates are only approximations, but they give you deadlines to aim for, and create a sense of urgency to get started, which is much better than the often-heard "someday, I'll" time frame.

Why set S.M.A.R.T. goals? Because they help you achieve your goals. They do this by making it easier to focus on what you need to do, help measure how well you're doing it, and provide a more definite and satisfying feeling of completion when you succeed.

Determining goals is one of the most important things you'll ever do. Your goals will shape your destiny. Take responsibility for setting goals that represent the best that is within you.

The quotes in this phase explore:

- Goals provide focus and clarity about what's important to you.

- Goals put you in control of your life.

- It takes courage and commitment to pursue your goals.

Instant Inspiration

Setting
Goals

If you have built castles in the air,
your work need not be lost;
that is where they should be.
Now put foundations under them.
Henry David Thoreau

All glory comes from daring to begin.
William Shakespeare

Begin somewhere:
you cannot build a reputation
on what you intend to do.
Liz Smith

The most important thing about goals
is having one.
Geoffry F. Abert

The indispensable first step
to getting the things you want out of life is this:
Decide what you want.
Ben Stein

Goals are simply a statement of
what your intentions are.
John Renesch

Beware what you set your heart upon,
for it shall surely be yours.
Ralph Waldo Emerson

Whatever we plant in our subconscious mind
and nourish with repetition and emotion
will one day become a reality.
Earl Nightingale

Where your talents and the world's needs cross,
there lies your vocation.
Aristotle

The important thing in life
is to have a great aim and to possess
the aptitude and the perseverance
to attain it.
Johann Wolfgang von Goethe

Every calling is great
when greatly pursued.
Oliver Wendell Holmes

You can't wait for inspiration.
You have to go after it with a club.
Jack London

The best time to plant a tree was 20 years ago.
The second best time is now.
Chinese Proverb

The discipline of writing something down
is the first step toward making it happen.
Lee Iacocca

Success is the continuous journey
towards the achievement of
predetermined, worthwhile goals.
Tom Hopkins

If you want to be successful;
it's just this simple.
Know what you are doing.
Love what you are doing.
And believe in what you are doing.
Will Rogers

Happiness, wealth, and success are
by-products of goal setting;
they cannot be the goals themselves.
John Condry

Goals are not only absolutely
necessary to motivate us.
They are essential to really keep us alive.
Robert Schuller

If you follow your bliss,
you put yourself on a track
that has been there all the while,
waiting for you.
Joseph Campbell

There is no medicine like hope,
no incentive so great,
and no tonic so powerful
as expectation of something better tomorrow.
Orison Swett Marden

The best way to predict the future
is to invent it.
Alan Kay

If you don't set goals for yourself,
you are doomed to work to achieve
the goals of somebody else.
Brian Tracy

Control your destiny or someone else will.
Jack Welch

There is one quality which one must possess to win,
and that is a definite purpose,
the knowledge of what one wants,
and a burning desire to possess it.
Napoleon Hill

They chose their paths not because they were easy,
but because they were difficult.
Mary Doria Russell

It's easy to make a buck.
It's a lot tougher to make a difference.
Tom Brokaw

Unless you try to do something beyond
what you have already mastered,
you will never grow.
Ronald Osborn

Many a man never fails
because he never tries.
Norman MacEwan

It is better to try and fail
than not to try and succeed.
Source Unknown

You miss 100 percent of the shots you never take.
Wayne Gretsky

The greatest danger for most of us
is not that our aim is too high and we miss it,
but that it is too low and we reach it.
Michelangelo

There is no guarantee of reaching
a goal at a certain time,
but there is a guarantee of never attaining
goals that are never set.
David McNally

People seldom hit what they do not aim at.
Henry David Thoreau

The tragedy of life doesn't lie
in not reaching your goal.
The tragedy lies in having no goal to reach.
Benjamin E. Mays

Most of us go to our graves
with our music still inside us.
Oliver Wendell Holmes

For all sad words,
of tongue and pen,
the saddest are these:
it might have been.
John Greenleaf Whittier

You may be disappointed if you fail,
but you will be doomed if you don't try.
Beverly Sills

Behold the turtle.
He makes progress only
when he sticks his neck out.
James Bryant Conant

No one ever achieved greatness
by playing it safe.
Harry Gray

The most rewarding things you do in life
are often the ones that look like
they cannot be done.
Arnold Palmer

Don't be afraid to take a big step if one is indicated.
You can't cross a chasm in two small jumps.
David Lloyd George

Accept the challenges,
so that you may feel
the exhilaration of victory.
George S. Patton

All life is an experiment.
The more experiments you make, the better.
Ralph Waldo Emerson

The future belongs to those who see possibilities
before they become obvious.
Theodore Levitt

Do the thing and you'll have the power.
Ralph Waldo Emerson

If we did all the things we are capable of doing,
we would literally astound ourselves.
Thomas Edison

Destiny is not a matter of chance,
it is a matter of choice;
it is not a thing to be waited for,
it is a thing to be achieved.
William Jennings Bryan

Don't ask yourself what the world needs.
Ask yourself what makes you come alive,
and go do that,
because what the world needs
is people who have come alive.
Howard Thurman

We achieve success, not by pursuing it,
but by finding the work which we enjoy
more than anything else,
and becoming the best in the world at it.
Thomas Jefferson

First say to yourself what you would be;
and then do what you have to do.
Epictetus

Don't bother just to be better
than your contemporaries or predecessors.
Try to be better than yourself.
William Faulkner

Our business in life
is not to get ahead of others,
but to get ahead of ourselves.
Stewart Johnson

You're in competition with one person only
and that is the individual you know you can become.
Martha Graham

My business is not to remake myself,
but make the absolute best of what God made.
Robert Browning

Only a mediocre person
is always at his best.
W. Somerset Maugham

Always be a first-rate version of yourself,
instead of a second-rate version of somebody else.
Judy Garland

The wise man travels to discover himself.
James Russell Lowell

I am not bound to win, I am bound to be true.
I am not bound to succeed,
but I am bound to live up to the light I have.
Abraham Lincoln

Hold yourself responsible for a higher standard
than anybody else expects of you.
Never excuse yourself.
Henry Ward Beecher

In the long run, we shape our lives,
and we shape ourselves.
The process never ends until we die.
And the choices we make
are ultimately our responsibility.
Eleanor Roosevelt

There is no tougher challenge that we face
than to accept personal responsibility
for not only what we are
but what we can be.
David McNally

Your ultimate goal in life
is to become your best self.
Your immediate goal is to get
on the path that will lead you there.
David Viscott

You are not here merely to make a living.
You are here in order to enable
the world to live more amply,
with genuine vision, with a finer spirit
of hope and achievement.
You are here to enrich the world,
and you impoverish yourself
if you forget the errand.
Woodrow Wilson

To have a great purpose to work for,
a purpose larger than ourselves,
is one of the secrets of making life significant;
for then the meaning and worth of the individual
overflow his personal borders,
and survive his death.
Will Durant

Don't concern yourself with how
you're going to achieve your goals.
Leave that to a power greater than yourself.
All you need to know is where you are going
and the answers will come to you.
Dorothea Brande

The task ahead of us is never as great
as the power behind us.
Ralph Waldo Emerson

I have dreamed my own self into being.
Alice Walker

Phase
Three

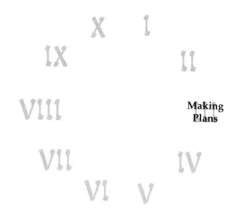

Making Plans

If goals are the road map to success, then making effective plans is the secret to achieving your goals. In this phase, you'll turn goal statements into operational plans—down to a level that you can schedule on a weekly and daily planner. Your detailed plans will spell out the logistics of achieving your goals: what you need to do; how you will accomplish it; who'll do what; when it'll be due; what obstacles you anticipate; and what additional resources you need.

After clarifying your dreams and goals, you need to identify intermediate steps that convert to monthly and weekly sub-goals, and, finally, break those down into daily tasks that you can schedule on your calendar. A critical procedure is to reduce plans into realistic, achievable chunks. Otherwise, you'll be overwhelmed.

Take 30 minutes every week to review goals and plans and establish weekly objectives for all the goals you're currently working on. By doing this, you keep moving forward and avoid living solely in crisis mode, where most of your time is spent addressing urgent deadlines and pressing obligations.

A final step is to take a few minutes at the end of every day to review goals and determine what you accomplished that day, then prioritize for tomorrow, based upon appointments and commitments. Doing this at day's end brings a sense of successful closure, cues up what you need to do tomorrow, and inspires a quick start the following morning.

It's important to realize that even with the best laid plans, nothing seems to go accordingly—and that's just the way life is. Re-evaluate and revise as you go. Practice being flexible and resilient with your goals. Flexibility is being able to accommodate changes to your plans; resiliency is being able to bounce back following a setback.

The majority of people never set goals, and that's why they fail to achieve anything extraordinary. Of those who do set goals, a large percentage fail to achieve them because they don't follow through on their plans. This is often caused by a failure to make plans that are detailed enough to track daily. You need to create steps so small that you can't help but achieve them. That's what is required to succeed.

The only way to achieve your goals is step by step. And it's a lot easier to take many small steps than a single giant leap. Are you ready?

The quotes in this phase explore:

- Planning is how you bring the future into the present.

- Good planning breaks big goals into manageable steps.

- Focus on achieving the few things that make the most impact.

Instant Inspiration

Making Plans

Plan for your future,
because that is where you're going
to spend the rest of your life.
Mark Twain

I expect to spend the rest of my life in the future
so I want to be reasonably sure
what kind of future it's going to be.
That is my reason for planning.
C. F. Kettering

Planning is bringing the future into the present
so that you can do something about it now.
Alan Lakein

Vision without action is just a dream.
Action without vision just passes the time.
Vision with action can change the world.
Loren Eiseley

Dreaming about a thing
in order to do it properly is right;
but dreaming about it
when we should be doing it is wrong.
Oswald Chambers

Great minds have purposes;
others have wishes.
Washington Irving

Make no small plans for
they have not the power to stir men's blood.
Niccolo Machiavelli

The only thing that stands between a man
and what he wants from life
is often merely the will to try it
and the faith to believe it is possible.
Richard M. DeVos

There is no scarcity of opportunity
to make a living at what you love to do,
there is only scarcity of resolve
to make it happen.
Wayne W. Dyer

If you want to get someplace,
you've got to give up wanting to get to that place;
in order to achieve something,
you've got to stop waiting for it to happen
and get into the process of achieving it.
Zen Proverb

It is not enough to be busy, so are the ants.
The question is, what are we busy about?
Henry David Thoreau

Visualize this thing you want.
See it, feel it, believe in it.
Make your mental blueprint,
and begin to build.
Robert Collier

You are never given a wish without also
being given the power to make it true.
You may have to work for it, however.
Richard Bach

Only those that risk going too far
can possibly know how far one can go.
T. S. Eliot

Make the most of your best.
Dorothy Sarnoff

Life shrinks or expands
in proportion to one's courage.
Anaïs Nin

Man cannot discover new oceans
unless he has courage
to lose sight of the shore.
Andre Gide

One man with courage is a majority.
Thomas Jefferson

Courage is the first of human qualities
because it is the quality
that guarantees all others.
Winston Churchill

You must have courage to bet on your ideals,
to take the calculated risk, and to act.
Everyday living requires courage
if life is to be effective and bring happiness.
Maxwell Maltz

Decide what you want,
decide what you are willing to exchange for it.
Establish your priorities and go to work.
H. L. Hunt

Take care of the means
and the end will take care of itself.
Mohandas K. Gandhi

The value of an idea
lies in the using of it.
Thomas Edison

Decision is the spark that ignites action.
Unless a decision is made, nothing happens.
Wilfred A. Peterson

It's so hard when contemplated in advance,
and so easy when you do it.
Robert Pirsig

A journey of a thousand miles
must begin with a single step.
Lao-Tzu

By the mile it's a trial;
by the yard it's hard;
but by the inch it's a cinch.
Zig Ziglar

All difficult things have their origin
in that which is easy,
all great things in that which is small.
Lao-Tzu

Always think of what you have to do
as easy and it will be.
Emile Coue

Making the simple complicated is commonplace;
making the complicated simple,
awesomely simple, that's creativity.
Charles Mingus

Nothing is particularly hard
if you divide it into small jobs.
Henry Ford

We think in generalities,
but we live in detail.
Alfred North Whitehead

God is in the details.
Mies van der Rohe

If you can't do great things,
do small things in a great way.
Don't wait for great opportunities.
Seize common, everyday ones
and make them great.
Napoleon Hill

You and I possess within ourselves,
at every moment of our lives,
under all circumstances,
the power to transform
the quality of our lives.
Werner Erhard

Often people attempt to live their lives backwards;
they try to have more things, or more money,
in order to do more of what they want,
so they will be happier.
The way it actually works is in reverse.
You must first be who you really are,
then do what you need to do,
in order to have what you want.
Margaret Young

Our plans miscarry because they have no aim.
When a man does not know what harbor
he is making for, no wind is the right wind.
Lucius Seneca

Men never plan to be failures;
they simply fail to plan to be successful.
William A. Ward

Those who fail to plan,
plan to fail.
George Hewell

You can never plan the future by the past.
Edmund Burke

If you do what you've always done,
you will get what you've always gotten.
Source Unknown

Almost as many individuals fail
because they try to do too much
as fail because they do not do enough.
J. Paul Getty

If you pursue two hares, both will escape you.
Greek Proverb

Who begins too much accomplishes little.
German Proverb

We have time enough
if we will but use it aright.
Johann Wolfgang von Goethe

A good plan today is better
than a great plan tomorrow.
George S. Patton

This time, like all times,
is a very good one,
if we but know what to do with it.
Ralph Waldo Emerson

All you have to do is know
where you're going.
The answers will come to you
of their own accord.
Earl Nightingale

Do not follow where the path may lead.
Go instead where there is no path and leave a trail.
Ralph Waldo Emerson

If you want to succeed, strike out on new paths
rather than travel the worn paths
of accepted success.
John D. Rockefeller

To do great and important tasks,
two things are necessary:
a plan and not quite enough time.
Source Unknown

Take time to deliberate,
but when the time for action has arrived,
stop thinking and go in.
Napoleon Bonaparte

Four steps to achievement:
Plan purposefully.
Prepare prayerfully.
Proceed positively.
Pursue persistently.
William A. Ward

Mastering life is the process of moving
from where you are to where you want to be.
Werner Erhard

People with goals succeed
because they know where they are going.
Earl Nightingale

A successful life does not result
from chance nor is it determined
by fate or good fortune,
but from a succession of successful days.
Ari Kiev

The important thing is this:
to be able at any moment
to sacrifice what we are
for what we could become.
Charles Du Bois

Everyone who got where he is
had to begin where he was.
Robert Louis Stevenson

Winning starts with beginning.
Robert Schuller

He has half the deed done
who has made a beginning.
Horace

All glory comes from daring to begin.
Eugene F. Ware

To change one's life:
Start immediately.
Do it flamboyantly.
No exceptions.
William James

Do not wait;
the time will never be 'just right.'
Start where you stand,
and work with whatever tools
you may have at your command,
and better tools will be found
as you go along.
Napoleon Hill

Until one is committed there is hesitancy,
the chance to draw back, always ineffectiveness.
Concerning all acts of initiative (and creation)
there is one elementary truth, the ignorance of which
kills countless ideas and splendid plans:
The moment one definitely commits oneself,
then Providence moves too.
All sorts of things occur to help one
that would otherwise never have occurred.
A whole stream of events issues from the decision,
raising in one's favor all manner
of unforeseen incidents and meetings
and material assistance, which no man
could have dreamed would have come his way.
W. H. Murray

Phase Four

X I
IX II
VIII III
VII
VI V

Aligning
Attitude

Aligning Attitude

Why is aligning attitude important enough to warrant its own phase? Because without the right attitude, striving for goals can degenerate into drudgery, just another entry on an endless "to-do" list. This is the wrong frame of mind for achieving goals and all but guarantees that you won't complete them.

What attitude helps you achieve goals? It's best summed up by the word "enthusiasm." This key word is derived from the Greek word *enthousiasmos*, which means "inspiration," which is derived from the root word *entheos*, meaning "God or spirit within."

By identifying goals you deeply desire and investing enthusiastic energy toward their fulfillment, you infuse actions with spirit and vitality. This powers a commitment to achieve the things you dearly want.

How do you achieve a peak level of enthusiasm? The inherent power of your goals can be a major motivator.

If goals represent things you deeply desire, then just spending time thinking about them and how they will improve your life will evoke powerful, positive emotions. These, in turn, generate motivational energy, which produces creative behavior.

Another simple way to create enthusiasm is to simply behave enthusiastically; just act "as if." Even if you don't feel enthusiastic but act more like you do, your thoughts and feelings will begin to follow. This phase directs the combined focus of your thoughts, feelings, and behaviors to the achievement of your goals. Goethe wrote, "It is astonishing what power our mind has over our body." Use the power of your mind to direct your "motions" (behaviors) and your emotions will follow.

Many people find using the technique of visualization very helpful. Visualizing is creating a mental movie of the future exactly as you want it to unfold. It is clearly picturing in your mind the end result, as well as each step necessary to achieve that result. Powerful goals evoke powerful mental pictures of success. The clearer the picture, the easier it is to "see" yourself achieving your goals. Your mind rehearses your success so that when you carry out your plans, it feels familiar and comfortable.

Another inner resource that helps with aligning attitude is "hope." It is the sustainer of all great dreams. You need to believe that you possess both the will and the way to accomplish your goals. Hope arises from your ability to motivate yourself when things are going well, but it is challenged when they aren't. To remain hopeful during difficult times requires being resourceful in finding creative ways around problems. It comes from deep conviction, optimism, and an expectation that you can and will achieve your goals no matter what.

The quotes in this phase explore:

- ■ Enthusiasm is the key to aligning attitude.

- ■ What you believe determines what you will achieve.

- ■ Visualizing your success helps to bring it about.

Instant Inspiration

Aligning Attitude

It is our attitude at the beginning
of a difficult undertaking which,
more than anything else,
will determine its successful outcome.
William James

Always bear in mind that your own resolution
to succeed is more important than any one thing.
Abraham Lincoln

I have begun everything
with the idea that I could succeed.
Booker T. Washington

If thou canst believe,
all things are possible
to him that believeth.
Bible, Mark 9:23

Strong convictions precede great actions.
J. F. Clarke

I have found enthusiasm for work
to be the most priceless ingredient
in any recipe for success.
Samuel Goldwyn

Enthusiasm is the mother of effort,
and without it nothing great was ever accomplished.
Ralph Waldo Emerson

Enthusiasm can only be aroused by two things:
first, an ideal which takes the imagination by storm—
and second, a definite intelligible plan
for carrying that ideal into practice.
Arnold Toynbee

A great attitude is not the result of success;
success is the result of a great attitude.
Earl Nightingale

A happy person is not a person
in a certain set of circumstances,
but rather a person with a
certain set of attitudes.
Hugh Downs

The greatest revelation of my generation
is the discovery that by changing
the inner attitudes of your mind,
you can change the outer aspects of your life.
William James

Success is a state of mind.
If you want success,
start thinking of yourself as a success.
Joyce Brothers

We must radiate success before it will come to us.
We must first become mentally,
from our attitude standpoint,
the people we wish to become.
Earl Nightingale

There is very little difference in people,
but that little difference makes a big difference.
The little difference is attitude.
The big difference is whether it is positive or negative.
W. Clement Stone

Nothing can stop the man
with the right mental attitude
from achieving his goal:
Nothing on earth can help the man
with the wrong mental attitude.
Thomas Jefferson

The most important words we'll ever utter
are those words we say to ourselves,
about ourselves, when we're by ourselves.
Al Walker

Your most important sale in life
is to sell yourself to yourself.
Maxwell Maltz

The man who cannot believe in himself
cannot believe in anything else.
Roy L. Smith

You must begin to think of yourself
as becoming the person you want to be.
David Viscott

One must not always think
so much about what one should do,
but rather what one should be.
Meister Eckhart

It all depends on how we look at things,
and not on how they are in themselves.
Carl Jung

What we see depends mainly
on what we look for.
John Lubbock

We do not see things as they are.
We see them as we are.
The Talmud

The meaning of things
lies not in the things themselves,
but in our attitude towards them.
Antoine de Saint-Exupery

Any fact facing us is not as important
as our attitude toward it,
for that determines our success or failure.
Norman Vincent Peale

If I have the belief that I can do it,
I shall surely acquire the capacity to do it
even if I may not have it at the beginning.
Mohandas K. Gandhi

Determine that the thing can and shall be done,
and then we shall find the way.
Abraham Lincoln

A strong passion for any object will ensure success,
for the desire of the end will point out the means.
William Hazlitt

It sometimes seems that intense desire
creates not only its own opportunities,
but its own talents.
Eric Hoffer

The mind is the limit.
As long as the mind can envision the fact
that you can do something,
you can do it—
as long as you really believe
one hundred percent.
Arnold Schwarzenegger

Our duty as men is to proceed
as if limits to our ability did not exist.
Pierre Teilhard de Chardin

There is nothing on earth you cannot have—
once you have mentally accepted
the fact that you can have it.
Robert Collier

That which you think today
becomes that which you are tomorrow.
Napoleon Hill

By your choice dwell you now
in the world which you have created.
What you hold in your heart shall be true,
and what most you admire,
that shall you become.
Richard Bach

Thought is the original source
of all wealth, all success, all material gain,
all great discoveries and inventions,
and of all achievement.
Claude M. Bristol

All that a man achieves
and all that he fails to achieve
is the direct result of his own thoughts.
James Allen

Our life always expresses
the result of our dominant thoughts.
Soren Kierkegaard

Every person is the creation of himself,
the image of his own thinking and believing.
Claude M. Bristol

The way we see events approaching us
affects the way we respond to them;
the way we respond to them
affects the way we regard ourselves;
and this in turn
affects the way we see new events.
W. Timothy Gallwey

The man who believes he can do it
is probably right,
and so is the man who believes he can't.
Laurence J. Peter

You are only limited by what your mind
has decided your limits will be.
John Renesch

Argue for your limitations
and sure enough, they're yours.
Richard Bach

We tend to get what we expect.
Norman Vincent Peale

It's not what you are that holds you back,
it's what you think you are not.
Denis Waitley

Times of change
are times of fearfulness
and times of opportunity.
Which they may be for you,
depends on your attitude toward them.
Ernest C. Smith

We should not let our fears
hold us back from pursuing our hopes.
John F. Kennedy

There is nothing in this world that's worth doing
that isn't going to scare you.
Barbara Sher

You win only if you aren't afraid to lose.
Rocky Aoki

The greatest mistake a man can make
is to be afraid of making one.
Elbert Hubbard

Failure is an attitude,
not an outcome.
Harvey MacKay

Our conduct is influenced
not by our experience
but by our expectations.
George Bernard Shaw

What we create within us
is always mirrored outside us.
Shakti Gawain

For things to change you've got to change.
Otherwise, nothing much will change.
Jim Rohn

Your past cannot be changed,
but you can change tomorrow
by your actions today.
David McNally

If you don't have the power to change yourself,
then nothing will change around you.
Anwar Sadat

One person with a belief
is equal to the force of ninety-nine.
John Stuart Mill

Self-confidence is the first
requisite to great undertakings.
Samuel Johnson

The important thing is to use today
wisely and well, and face tomorrow
eagerly and cheerfully
and with the certainty that we shall
be equal to what it brings.
Channing Pollock

You can do very little with faith,
but you can do nothing without it.
Samuel Butler

Faith is to believe
what we do not see;
and the reward of this faith
is to see what we believe.
Saint Augustine

Faith is the substance of things hoped for,
the evidence of things not seen.
Bible, Hebrews 11:1

Each day you have to look in the mirror
and say to yourself,
'I'm going to be the best I can
no matter what it takes.'
Barbara Jordan

The best are not motivated by money,
but by the desire to be the best.
Denis Waitley

The mind is not a vessel to be filled
but a fire to be ignited.
Plutarch

Success isn't a result of spontaneous combustion.
You must set yourself on fire.
Arnold Glascow

Life is too short to be little.
Man is never so manly
as when he feels deeply,
acts boldly, and expresses himself
with frankness and with fervor.
Benjamin Disraeli

They are able who think they are able.
Virgil

Nurture your minds with great thoughts.
To believe in the heroic makes heroes.
Benjamin Disraeli

Nothing in this world is impossible
to a willing heart.
Abraham Lincoln

Every man is free to rise
as far as he's able or willing,
but it's only the degree to which
he thinks that determines
the degree to which he'll rise.
Ayn Rand

A man is what he thinks about all day long.
Ralph Waldo Emerson

Our life is what our thoughts make it.
Marcus Aurelius

A picture is an intermediate something
between a thought and a thing.
Calvin Coolidge

Picture yourself vividly as winning,
and that alone will contribute
immeasurably to success.
Harry Emerson Fosdick

Visualizing something organizes
one's ability to accomplish it.
Stephen R. Covey

See things as you would have them be
instead of as they are.
Robert Collier

If you want to reach a goal,
you must see the reaching in your own mind
before you actually arrive at your goal.
Zig Ziglar

You merely picture in your mind
having already accomplished
or attained your goal,
whatever it may be.
Hold it firmly in your thoughts,
picture it as already being yours,
and amazing things will happen.
Og Mandino

Change your thoughts
and you change your world.
Norman Vincent Peale

Phase
Five

X   I

IX   II

VIII   III

VII   IV

VI   V

Disciplining
Action

Disciplining Action

After you've cultivated your dreams, set your goals, made your plans, and aligned your attitude, "sooner or later, all the thinking and planning has to degenerate to work," as Peter Drucker writes. There's no avoiding it: Success requires disciplined action. This is where many stumble with their goals.

There's a psychological principle that helps discipline actions for success. Focus on the small positive progress you make every day and don't pay attention to what you don't accomplish. Too often, for a variety of reasons, we get discouraged because we aren't moving as fast as we would like. This negative approach discounts everything we are doing, and leaves us feeling down. In this state of mind, it's easy to abandon our goals.

You may want to make notes about what you do on your goals each day. It's important to record any action that moves you in the right direction, no matter how small, and to feel good about your forward progress. With disciplining action, it's really a matter of "slow and steady wins the race." Remember, it isn't how fast you're going, it's what direction you're headed.

The essence of this phase is forming habits that reinforce your commitment to your goals. Habits are behaviors that you perform so often that they become automatic. The way to form good goal habits is to keep your goals in front of you at all times. Signs, reminders, and sticky notes all help you focus on the importance of your goals. Even in the midst of appointments, deadlines, and countless other interruptions, carve out a little time each day to move your goals forward. This can be difficult, but you can make it your personal challenge, the dues you pay for achieving real success.

As you've no doubt learned from past attempts at personal improvement, such as losing weight, getting in shape, or reducing stress, it's a lot easier to maintain a habit (even at a minimal level) than it is to start and stop, time after time. So how can you maintain and grow good habits every day to build the disciplined action you need to succeed? An obvious suggestion is to identify one thing (even a small accomplishment) every day that qualifies as a step toward your goal and do it as early in the day as possible. Write it down, get it done, check it off. Make this one step a daily habit, a personal commitment, a promise to yourself and to your success.

The quotes in this phase explore:

- Plans must be translated into actions.
- Many small steps lead to big results.
- Your habits will either make or break your success.

Disciplining Action

Good thoughts are no better than good dreams,
unless they be executed.
Ralph Waldo Emerson

If we want to live healthy lives,
we have to build into our daily life
moments of vision and then
let our action be formed by that vision.
David Steindl-Rast

Acting on a good idea is better
than just having a good idea.
Robert Half

Any powerful idea is absolutely fascinating
and absolutely useless until we choose to use it.
Richard Bach

Everyone who's ever taken a shower
has had an idea.
But it's the person who gets out of the shower,
dries off, and does something with his idea
who makes a difference.
Nolan Bushnell

The world can only be grasped by action,
not by contemplation.
Jacob Bronowski

The actions of men are the best interpreters
of their thoughts.
John Locke

You make the path by walking.
Robert Bly

The smallest good deed is better
than the grandest good intention.
Joseph Duquet

Movement is the essence of life.
It is also the embodiment of intention—
the intention of the individual.
Moshe Feldenkrais

Trust only movement.
Life happens at the level of events not of words.
Alfred Adler

Seize the day;
put no trust in the morrow.
Horace

Opportunities multiply as they are seized.
Sun Tzu

You can't build a reputation on
what you're going to do.
Henry Ford

Success is turning knowledge
into positive action.
Dorothy Leeds

Success is making the most
of the best that is within you every day
by having a goal, being committed to it,
and underscoring it with enthusiasm.
Al Walker

You've got to be before you can do,
and you've got to do before you can have.
Zig Ziglar

Do what you can, with what you have,
where you are.
Theodore Roosevelt

We cannot put off living until we are ready.
The most salient characteristic of life
is its coerciveness: it is always urgent,
"here and now"
without any possible postponement.
Life is fired at us point blank.
Jose Ortega y Gasset

Seek this very minute, whatever you can do,
or dream you can, begin it.
Boldness has genius, power and magic in it.
Only engage and the mind grows heated,
begin and the task will be completed.
Johann Wolfgang von Goethe

Begin; to begin is half the work.
Let half still remain;
again, begin this,
and thou wilt have finished.
Ansonius

Besides the noble art of getting things done,
master the noble art of leaving things undone.
The wisdom of life consists
in the elimination of nonessentials.
Lin Yutang

To gain knowledge, add some every day.
To gain wisdom, get rid of something every day.
Lao-Tzu

To be really great in the little things,
to be truly noble and heroic
in the insipid details of everyday life,
is a virtue so rare as to be
worthy of canonization.
Harriet Beecher Stowe

There usually are half a dozen answers
to 'What needs to be done?'
Yet unless a man makes the risky
and controversial choice of only one,
he will achieve nothing.
Peter F. Drucker

To know what has to be done, then do it,
comprises the whole philosophy of practical life.
Sir William Osler

The quickest way to do many things
is to do only one thing at a time.
Irish Proverb

Accomplish the great task
by a series of small acts.
Lao-Tzu

We cannot do everything at once,
but we can do something at once.
Calvin Coolidge

Accomplishment of a goal takes a very little time
when energy is focused on specific action.
Source Unknown

For purposes of action
nothing is more useful
than narrowness of thought
combined with energy of will.
Henri Frederic Amiel

When every physical and mental resource is focused,
one's power to solve a problem
multiplies tremendously.
Norman Vincent Peale

Think like a man of action,
act like a man of thought.
Henri Bergson

Wisdom oftimes consists
of knowing what to do next.
Herbert Hoover

The secret of success in life
is for a man to be ready
for his time when it comes.
Benjamin Disraeli

Success doesn't come to you…
you go to it.
Marva Collins

Some people dream of worthy accomplishments,
while others stay awake and do them.
Source Unknown

Start by doing what's necessary,
then what's possible,
and suddenly you are doing the impossible.
Saint Francis of Assisi

Pray as if everything depended on God,
and work as if everything depended on you.
Francis Cardinal Spellman

The soul's joy lives in doing.
Percy Bysshe Shelley

I think that one must finally take
one's life into one's hands.
Arthur Miller

I am only one, but still I am one;
I cannot do everything, but still I can do something;
I will not refuse to do the something I can do.
Helen Keller

No man can know what he can do until he tries.
Publilius Syrus

The only difference between those
who have failed and those who have succeeded
lies in the difference of their habits.
Good habits are the key to all success.
Bad habits are the unlocked door to failure.
Og Mandino

Excellence is an act won by training and habituation.
We do not act rightly because we have
virtue or excellence, but rather we have those
because we have acted rightly.
We are what we repeatedly do.
Excellence then, is not an act, but a habit.
Aristotle

The nature of man is always the same;
it is their habits that separate them.
Confucius

We first make our habits,
and then our habits make us.
John Dryden

The chains of habit are too weak to be felt
until they are too strong to be broken.
Samuel Johnson

Habits are like a cable.
We weave a strand of it everyday,
and soon it cannot be broken.
Horace Mann

Cultivate only the habits that
you are willing should master you.
Elbert Hubbard

No life grows great until it is
focused, dedicated, disciplined.
Harry Emerson Fosdick

Without discipline, there is no life at all.
Katherine Hepburn

All excellence involves discipline
and tenacity of purpose.
John W. Gardner

For every disciplined effort
there is a multiple reward.
Jim Rohn

Labor is still, and ever will be,
the inevitable price set upon
everything which is valuable.
Samuel Smiles

The quality of a person's life
is in direct proportion
to their commitment to excellence,
regardless of their chosen field of endeavor.
Vincent Lombardi

If you don't do it excellently, don't do it at all.
Because if it's not excellent,
it won't be profitable or fun,
and if you're not in the business for fun or profit,
what the hell are you doing there?
Robert Townsend

One of the rarest things
that a man ever does
is to do the best he can.
Josh Billings

A strong will, a settled purpose,
an invincible determination,
can accomplish almost anything.
Thomas Fuller

There is no such thing as a great talent
without great will power.
Honore de Balzac

Nothing is impossible;
there are ways that lead to everything,
and if we had sufficient will
we should always have sufficient means.
It is often merely for an excuse
that we say things are impossible.
Francois de La Rochefoucauld

Many people think they want things,
but they don't really have the strength, the discipline.
They are weak.
I believe that you get what you want
if you want it badly enough.
Sophia Loren

You have to understand what it is
that you are better at than anybody else
and mercilessly focus your efforts on it.
Andrew Grove

Choose a job you love,
and you will never have to work
a day in your life.
Confucius

Nothing is really work
unless you would rather
be doing something else.
James M. Barrie

The minute you begin to do what you really want to do,
it's really a different kind of life.
Buckminster Fuller

Do your job naturally because you like it
and success will take care of itself.
Norman Vincent Peale

When love and skill work together,
expect a miracle.
John Ruskin

I will act as if what I do makes a difference.
William James

Each of our acts makes a statement
as to our purpose.
Leo Buscaglia

Action may not always bring happiness
but there is no happiness without action.
Benjamin Disraeli

There are risks and costs
to a program of action.
But they are far less than
the long range risks and costs
of comfortable inaction.
John F. Kennedy

Even if you're on the right track,
you'll get run over if you just sit there.
Will Rogers

Everything comes to him who
hustles while he waits.
Thomas Edison

We learn to do something by doing it.
There is no other way.
John Holt

I know of no more encouraging fact
than the unquestionable ability of man
to elevate his life by conscious effort.
Henry David Thoreau

We must use time wisely and forever realize that
the time is always ripe to do right.
Nelson Mandela

Action should culminate in wisdom.
Bhagavad-Gita

The dictionary is the only place
that success comes before work.
Vincent Lombardi

Phase Six

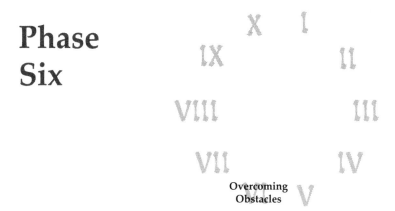

Overcoming Obstacles

Obstacles to your goals are nuisances in what has been, up to this point, an interesting and inspiring journey. Some obstacles are small and easy to handle, while others are significant and require everything you've got to manage them. Regardless of the size or the form, it is your attitude about the obstacles that determines whether you overcome or succumb to them.

The truth about most goal-related obstacles is that they are natural and inevitable by-products of growth and change and accompany the pursuit of all important goals. To manage them you should always adopt a creative, problem-solving approach. If you personalize them, deny or resist them, or feel victimized or righteous about them, you will stall your forward progress. All of those reactions lead you farther away from your goals.

Obstacles usually highlight when there's a need for new knowledge, skills, or perspective. They often mean you're trying to solve new situations using outmoded strategies. Taking a training class, learning the latest technology, or talking with an expert may be all that's needed to move past the hurdle. Sometimes, however, they indicate there's a need to recommit to your goals at a deeper level or, perhaps, reconsider whether it is still an important goal.

Regardless of the obstacle or its source, you need to realize the importance of being able to plan for all kinds of tests and challenges to your goals. Some are anticipated while others catch you totally by surprise. It doesn't matter. Contingency planning is a "survival skill" for goal achievement.

Obstacles come in two forms: external and internal. External obstacles are those constraints that exist outside of yourself and impede your progress towards your goals. Such things as insufficient time, work responsibilities and limited finances are all realistic external obstacles that impact your goals.

Internal obstacles are those that you create for yourself by your thinking and by the limitations you put on yourself. These often involve your self-image and what you imagine is and is not possible for you to achieve. Internal obstacles are more difficult to recognize and rectify, and they sometimes require the help of an outside coach to overcome them.

Great goal achievers are not without great obstacles. They achieve great things because they overcome their obstacles with proactive responses and a confident attitude. They know that the way they handle adversity determines how long it will be before they ultimately succeed. And they also know that the achievements that mean the most are the ones they had to work hardest to win.

The quotes in this phase explore:

- All great goals require overcoming obstacles.

- Your ability to manage obstacles determines your level of success.

- Your challenge is to turn obstacles into opportunities.

Instant Inspiration

Overcoming Obstacles

Successful people are not people without problems;
they're simply people who've learned
to solve their problems.
Robert Seashore

I have learned that success is to be measured
not so much by the position that one has reached
in life as by the obstacles that
he has overcome while trying to succeed.
Booker T. Washington

The ultimate measure of a man
is not where he stands in moments
of comfort and convenience,
but where he stands at times
of challenge and controversy.
Martin Luther King, Jr.

Success is not measured
by what a man accomplishes,
but by the opposition he has encountered,
and the courage with which
he has maintained the struggle
against overwhelming odds.
Charles A. Lindbergh

Nothing stops the man who desires to achieve.
Every obstacle is simply a course
to develop his achievement muscle.
It's a strengthening of his powers of accomplishment.
Eric Butterworth

History has demonstrated that the most
notable winners usually encountered heartbreaking
obstacles before they triumphed.
They won because they refused
to become discouraged by their defeats.
B. C. Forbes

Obstacles are what we see
when we take our eyes off our goal.
As long as we're focused on
what we're striving to achieve,
obstacles aren't obstacles anymore;
they're problems to be solved,
one by one, as they appear in our path.
Earl Nightingale

Obstacles in the pathway of the weak
become the stepping stones
in the pathway of the strong.
Thomas Carlyle

Obstacles will look large or small to you
according to whether you are large or small.
Orison Swett Marden

The greater the obstacle,
the more glory in overcoming it.
Jean-Baptiste Moliere

If there is no struggle, there is no progress.
Frederick Douglass

What is easy is seldom excellent.
Samuel Johnson

If you find a path with no obstacles,
it probably doesn't lead anywhere.
Frank A. Clark

All difficult things have their origin
in that which is easy,
and great things in that which is small.
Lao-Tzu

A problem is a chance for you to do your best.
Duke Ellington

Where you stumble,
there your treasure lies.
Joseph Campbell

There is no education like adversity.
Benjamin Disraeli

It may not be your fault for being down,
but it's got to be your fault for not getting up.
Steve Davis

It's not whether you get knocked down,
it's whether you get up.
Vincent Lombardi

The thing we call failure is not in falling down—
it's in staying down.
Mary Pickford

That which does not kill me makes me stronger.
Friedrich Nietzche

What the caterpillar calls the end of the world,
the master calls a butterfly.
Richard Bach

The biggest obstacle between us and our goals
is a lack of total commitment.
Wally Amos

My life has been one long obstacle course
with me as the biggest obstacle.
Jack Paar

People spend most of their lives worrying
about things that never happen.
Jean-Baptiste Moliere

Nothing will ever be attempted
if all possible obstacles must first be overcome.
Samuel Johnson

You must do the thing you think you cannot do.
Eleanor Roosevelt

One of the great discoveries a man makes,
one of his great surprises,
is to find he can do
what he was afraid he couldn't do.
Henry Ford

One of the reasons mature people stop learning
is that they become less and less
willing to risk failure.
John W. Gardner

And the trouble is,
if you don't risk anything,
you risk even more.
Erica Jong

Progress always involves risk;
you can't steal second base
and keep your foot on first.
Frederick Wilcox

A person who's trying to achieve
the pleasure of success
without ever experiencing
the pain of rejection
will never succeed long term.
Anthony Robbins

If one will attempt
the most difficult endeavor
his mind can possibly conceive
and is successful in that venture,
then for the rest of his life,
everything else will seem
easy by comparison.
Friedrich Nietzche

Adversity causes some men to break;
others to break records.
William A. Ward

Barriers are invitations to courage.
Source Unknown

Courage is resistance to fear,
mastery of fear—
not absence of fear.
Mark Twain

True success is overcoming
the fear of being unsuccessful.
Paul Sweeney

I have not ceased being fearful,
but I have ceased to let fear control me.
Erica Jong

The man who fears suffering
is already suffering for what he fears.
Michel de Montaigne

Do what you fear and fear disappears.
David Joseph Schwartz

One who fears failure limits his worth.
Failure is the opportunity
to begin again more intelligently.
Henry Ford

Failure is the best guarantee
of future success.
To fail, we have to try to do something.
This in itself is an achievement,
regardless of the outcome.
Earl Nightingale

The successful man will profit
from his mistakes and try again
in a different way.
Dale Carnegie

Anyone who has never been disappointed
has set his sights too low.
Robert Schuller

If at first you don't succeed,
you're running about average.
M. H. Alderson

How you think when you lose
determines how long it will be
until you win.
David Joseph Schwartz

Loss, by itself, is not tragic.
What is tragic is the failure to grasp
the opportunity which loss presents.
Robert Greenleaf

The person interested in success
has to learn to view failure
as a healthy, inevitable part
of the process of getting to the top.
Joyce Brothers

You can't succeed if you don't fail sometimes.
But if you're not prepared for failure,
it's going to take you by surprise
and knock you for a loop.
So you have to manage with the understanding
that things may not work out according to plan.
You have to have your strategy backed up.
The secret is to make contingency planning
a habit of mind.
Jack Stack

We are continually faced
with great opportunities
brilliantly disguised as
insolvable problems.
Ann Landers

It still holds true that man is most uniquely human
when he turns obstacles into opportunities.
Eric Hoffer

Every situation, properly perceived,
becomes an opportunity.
Helen Schucman

People like you and me may become giants.
Giants see opportunity where others see trouble.
Max DePree

Out of clutter, find simplicity.
From discord, find harmony.
In the middle of difficulty lies opportunity.
Albert Einstein

Problems are not stop signs; they are guidelines.
Robert Schuller

I am not discouraged,
because every wrong attempt discarded
is another step forward.
Thomas Edison

You must have long-range goals
to keep you from being frustrated
by short-term failure.
Charles C. Noble

Notice the difference between what happens
when a man says to himself, 'I have failed three times,'
and what happens when he says, 'I am a failure.'
S. I. Hayakawa

There are two ways of meeting difficulties:
you alter the difficulties
or you alter yourself to meet them.
Source Unknown

Not everything that is faced can be changed,
but nothing can be changed until it is faced.
James Baldwin

Don't let what you cannot do
interfere with what you can do.
John Wooden

Some men have thousands of reasons
why they cannot do what they want to,
when all they need is one reason
why they can.
Willis R. Whitney

It is not because things are difficult
that we do not dare;
it is because we do not dare
that things are difficult.
Lucius Seneca

How many a man has thrown up his hands
at a time when a little more effort,
a little more patience,
would have achieved success.
Elbert Hubbard

The deepest personal defeat
suffered by human beings
is constituted by the difference between
what one was capable of becoming
and what one has in fact become.
Ashley Montagu

Far better to dare mighty things,
to win glorious triumphs,
even though checkered by failure,
than to take rank with those poor spirits
who neither enjoy much nor suffer much,
because they live in the gray twilight
that knows not victory, nor defeat.
Theodore Roosevelt

People are always blaming their circumstances
for what they are.
I don't believe in circumstances.
The people who get on in this world
are the people who get up
and look for the circumstances they want,
and, if they can't find them, make them.
George Bernard Shaw

It's the constant and determined effort
that breaks down all resistance,
sweeps away all obstacles.
Claude M. Bristol

The gem cannot be polished without friction,
nor man perfected without trials.
Confucius

Conquering any difficulty always gives one a secret joy,
for it means pushing back a boundary line
and adding to one's liberty.
Henri Frederic Amiel

All life is the struggle,
the effort to be itself.
The difficulties which I meet with
in order to realize my existence
are precisely what awaken
and mobilize my activities,
my capabilities.
Jose Ortega y Gasset

In every adversity, there is the seed
of an equivalent or greater benefit.
Napoleon Hill

The way I see it,
if you want the rainbow,
you gotta put up with the rain.
Dolly Parton

Pray not for a lighter load,
but for stronger shoulders.
Saint Augustine

What looks like a loss
may be the very event
which is subsequently responsible
for helping to produce
the major achievement of your life.
Srully Blotnick

Phase Seven

X I
IX II
VIII III
Reinforcing
Accomplishments IV
VII
VI V

Reinforcing Accomplishments

Basic psychology tells us behavior that's reinforced tends to be repeated. The opposite is also true: behavior that's not reinforced tends not to be continued. In terms of goals, it's important to recognize all positive steps and accomplishments so you repeat them again and again.

This is critical because, very often, the actions you need to accomplish goals are new behaviors that break old habits, and you have a strong tendency to fall back into old patterns unless you immediately reinforce the new ones. In other words, don't wait to reach your destination before you celebrate your accomplishments; cement them immediately and repeatedly.

Reinforcement can be tangible or intangible and can come from other people or as something you give yourself. Examples of tangible reinforcements coming from others are a spot bonus, a plaque, or a pin. Intangibles coming from others are when friends praise you or take you out to celebrate a milestone accomplishment. Treating yourself to a new CD or a pair of shoes are examples of tangible reinforcements you give to yourself. Intangible reinforcements are your feelings of pride, joy, or satisfaction about accomplishing something important. It may be the sheer joy of working hard at a job you love to do.

Just as planned stops on a long car trip break up the driving, planned reinforcements on the journey to your goals can make the trip much more rewarding. Decide what rewards you value and plan your "treats" along the way to make each milestone more motivating.

Remember, success doesn't come in big sweeping break-throughs. It comes gradually in a series of small victories, achieved one after another, over a prolonged period of time. In order to maintain the momentum necessary to sustain high levels of energy and enthusiasm, reinforcement is required. Accept it from others when they offer it, but most importantly, learn to give it to yourself, frequently and abundantly.

The quotes in this phase explore:

- Celebrate small accomplishments to your goals.

- Stay focused on the work you need to do right now.

- Enjoy the journey to success as much as the destination.

Reinforcing
Accomplishments

Nothing succeeds like success.
Alexandre Dumas, the Elder

The world has the habit of making room
for the man whose words and actions
show that he knows where he is going.
Napoleon Hill

I find the great thing in this world
is not so much where we stand,
as in what direction we are moving.
Oliver Wendell Holmes

It is not the attainment of the goal that matters,
it is the things that are met with along the way.
Havelock Ellis

Powerful people know that
getting there is all the fun.
Nancy Anderson

Men acquire a particular quality
by constantly acting in a particular way.
Aristotle

Sow a thought, and you reap an act.
Sow an act, and you reap a habit.
Sow a habit, and you reap a character.
Sow a character, and you reap a destiny.
Source Unknown

What we love we shall grow to resemble.
Bernard of Clairvaux

Have patience with all things,
but chiefly have patience with yourself.
Do not lose courage in considering
your own imperfections,
but instantly set about remedying them.
Everyday begin the task anew.
Saint Francis de Sales

People who are unable to motivate themselves
must be content with mediocrity,
no matter how impressive their other talents.
Andrew Carnegie

You are only one thought away
from a good feeling.
Sheila Krystal

We lift ourselves by our thoughts,
we climb upon our vision of ourselves.
Orison Swett Marden

What I am today is more a result
of what I am becoming
than what I have been in the past.
Source Unknown

Day by day, in every way,
I'm getting better and better.
Emile Coue

Success is the sum of small efforts
repeated day in and day out.
Robert Collier

Practice yourself, for heaven's sake,
in little things;
and thence proceed to greater.
Epictetus

You've got to think about 'big things'
while you're doing small things
so that the small things
go in the right direction.
Alvin Toffler

We must not, in trying to think about
how we can make a difference,
ignore the small daily differences we can make,
which, over time, add up to big differences
we cannot foresee.
Marian Wright Edelman

Each small task of everyday life
is part of the total harmony of the universe.
Saint Theresa of Lisieux

Growth itself contains the germ of happiness.
Pearl S. Buck

Be not afraid of growing slowly,
be afraid only of standing still.
Chinese Proverb

The only true security in life
comes from knowing that
every single day you are
improving yourself in some way.
Anthony Robbins

One learns by doing a thing;
for though you think you know it,
you have no certainty until you try.
Sophocles

Better to do something imperfectly
than to do nothing flawlessly.
Robert Schuller

Nothing would be done at all
if a man waited until he could do it
so well that no one could find fault with it.
Cardinal Newman

If you want to increase your success rate,
double your failure rate.
Thomas J. Watson, Sr.

Winners focus on past successes
and forget past failures.
Denis Waitley

What we think or what we know or believe
is, in the end, of little consequence.
The only consequence is what we do.
John Ruskin

Some of us will do our jobs well
and some will not,
but we will all be judged
by only one thing—
the results.
Vincent Lombardi

Perhaps the most valuable result of all education
is the ability to make yourself do the thing you have to do,
when it ought to be done, whether you like it or not;
it is the first lesson that ought to be learned,
and however early a man's training begins,
it is probably the last lesson he learns thoroughly.
Thomas Henry Huxley

There is no substitute for hard work.
Thomas Edison

Make your work to be in keeping with your purpose.
Leonardo da Vinci

The most satisfying happiness
known to man is to create something;
to sit and be impressed
by the creations of other people
is only a second-rate kind of happiness.
Harry Emerson Fosdick

Keep doing whatever gives you
inner help and comfort.
Give up only what no longer
has any attraction to you,
or interferes with
something greatly desired.
Mohandas K. Gandhi

Excellence is to do a common thing
in an uncommon way.
Booker T. Washington

Pleasure in the job
puts perfection in the work.
Aristotle

Your chances of success are directly
proportional to the degree of pleasure
you derive from what you do.
Michael Korda

Work joyfully and peacefully,
knowing that right thoughts and right efforts
will inevitably bring about right results.
James Allen

Luck is what happens when
preparation meets opportunity.
Elmer Letterman

In order that people may be happy in their work,
these three things are needed:
they must be fit for it,
they must not do too much of it,
and they must have a sense of success in it.
John Ruskin

Everyone has noted
the astonishing sources of energy
that seem available to those
who enjoy what they are doing
or find meaning in what they are doing.
Charles Garfield

On this and every turn,
we'll be making progress and
progress is not just moving ahead.
Progress is dreaming, working,
building a better way of life.
Walt Disney

The man who does not work for the love of work,
but only for money
is neither likely to make money
nor to find much fun in life.
Charles M. Schwab

There must be more to life than having everything.
Maurice Sendak

Work is not man's punishment.
It is his reward and his strength and his pleasure.
George Sand

To love what you do and feel that it matters—
how could anything be more fun?
Katherine Graham

We act as though comfort and luxury
were the chief requirements of life
when all that we need to make us really happy
is something to be enthusiastic about.
Charles Kingsley

Whenever anything is being accomplished
it is being done by a monomaniac with a mission.
Peter F. Drucker

To keep a lamp burning,
we have to keep putting oil in it.
Mother Teresa

One reason we don't attain our goals
is that we often focus on how far away
we are from feeling satisfaction
rather than how far we've come.
Fred Pryor

No one keeps up his enthusiasm automatically.
Enthusiasm must be nourished with new actions,
new aspirations, new efforts, new vision.
It is one's own fault if his enthusiasm is gone.
He has failed to feed it.
Source Unknown

Plenty of people miss their share of happiness,
not because they never found it,
but because they didn't stop to enjoy it.
William Feather

Celebrate what you want to see more of.
Tom Peters

To do today's work well
and not to be bothered about tomorrow
is the secret of accomplishment.
Sir William Osler

Phase Eight

Developing
Perseverance

Developing Perseverance

Goal-setting success comes down to perseverance, which is the heart and soul of achievement. In the crush of deadlines, distractions, and disappointments, it takes commitment and focus to keep goals alive and moving forward. Great goals take great effort over a long period.

There's no magic to developing perseverance. Techniques can help (see the Ten-Step Action Plan, page 169) but the bottom line is character, which makes this the hardest of the phases to develop. You have to eliminate the word "quit" from your vocabulary if you want to achieve your goals.

Let's distinguish between quitting and backsliding. Quitting is abandoning your goals, whereas backsliding is a temporary relapse into old behavior. All of us will backslide when attempting to make significant changes in our lives. This is natural. We resist moving beyond what is familiar and comfortable. This should be seen as part of the bigger process. What is critical about backsliding is that it shouldn't cause you to abandon your goals. The road to success is never a straight one. Just acknowledge and accept the slide as a temporary detour and correct your course as quickly as possible.

Perseverance is achieved by developing regular habits that move you in the direction of your goals. Be patient with yourself, realizing that you neither drop bad habits nor acquire better ones in a day (or even a week). Give yourself permission not to have to do things right the first time. Taking the long view and looking for continual progress is always a better approach than expecting perfection. One reason perseverance is the hardest phase to develop is that learning to be patient with yourself is often a lifelong education. It is a mental muscle that grows stronger with regular use.

We live in a world of instant gratification, making it difficult to develop perseverance. Achieving great things doesn't happen immediately, so we run short on patience. In order to develop perseverance, you have to give up the idea of completing goals instantly and learn to enjoy the continuous process of unfolding and learning. To return again and again to the work at hand is to master the discipline of "one step at a time." If you learn to take several enjoyable steps today, there's a likelihood that you'll want to return tomorrow to take several more, and that's developing perseverance.

The quotes in this phase explore:

- Excellence can only be achieved after great efforts.

- Character is the inner source that sustains perseverance.

- Genius is mostly just the power of perseverance.

VIII
Developing Perseverance

Success in life is a matter
not so much of talent or opportunity
as of concentration and perseverance.
C. W. Wendte

With ordinary talent
and extraordinary perseverance,
all things are attainable.
Thomas Buxton

Successful people are just ordinary people
with an extraordinary amount of
persistence and determination.
Source Unknown

The difference between ordinary
and extraordinary is that little "extra."
Source Unknown

Let me tell you the secret
that has led me to my goal.
My strength lies solely in my tenacity.
Louis Pasteur

I do not think there is any other
so essential to success of any kind
as the quality of perseverance.
It overcomes almost everything, even nature.
John D. Rockefeller

When you get right down to the root
of the meaning of the word, "succeed,"
you find that it simply means to follow through.
F. W. Nichol

I know the price of success—
dedication, hard work,
and the unremitting devotion
to the things you want to see happen.
Frank Lloyd Wright

Nothing in the world can
take the place of persistence.
Talent will not;
nothing is more common than
unsuccessful men with talent.
Genius will not;
unrewarded genius is almost a proverb.
Education will not;
the world is full of educated derelicts.
Persistence and determination alone are omnipotent.
Calvin Coolidge

Energy and persistence conquer all things.
Benjamin Franklin

Self-discipline is the ability to make yourself
do what you should do,
when you should do it,
whether you feel like it or not.
Elbert Hubbard

When you do the things you need to do
when you ought to do them,
the day will come when you can do
the things you want to do
when you want to do them.
Robert Anthony

People who get ahead are those
who prove they can get things done.
David Kearns

The difference between a successful person
and others is not a lack of strength,
not a lack of knowledge,
but rather a lack of will.
Vincent Lombardi

Nothing resists a human will
that stakes its very existence
upon the achievement of its purpose.
Benjamin Disraeli

We can do anything we want to do
if we stick to it long enough.
Helen Keller

The greatest pleasure in life
is doing what people say you cannot do.
Walter Bagehot

When a man has put a limit
on what he will do,
he has put a limit on what he can do.
Charles M. Schwab

Today I do what others won't,
so that tomorrow I do what others can't.
Source Unknown

Any time you stop striving to get better,
you're bound to get worse.
Pat Riley

He who stops being better
stops being good.
Oliver Cromwell

Whatever you are by nature, keep to it;
never desert your line of talent.
Be what nature intended you for,
and you will succeed.
Sydney Smith

Slow and steady wins the race.
Aesop

Little strokes fell great oaks.
Benjamin Franklin

One man has enthusiasm for 30 minutes,
another for 30 days,
but it is the man who has it for 30 years
who makes a success of his life.
Edward B. Butler

It takes twenty years
to make an overnight success.
Eddie Cantor

Excellence in any department can be attained
only by the labor of a lifetime;
it is not to be purchased at a lesser price.
Samuel Johnson

In most things success depends
on knowing how long it takes to succeed.
Charles Baron de Montesquieu

Our greatest weakness lies in giving up.
The most certain way to succeed
is always to try just one more time.
Thomas Edison

Success seems to be largely a matter of
hanging on after others have let go.
William Feather

When you get into a tight place
and it seems you can't go on,
hang on, for that's just the place and the time
that the tide will turn.
Harriet Beecher Stowe

In the midst of winter,
I finally learned that there was
in me an invincible summer.
Albert Camus

The world breaks everyone,
then some become strong at the broken places.
Ernest Hemingway

Don't wish it were easier;
wish you were better.
Jim Rohn

It is better to live one day as a lion
than a hundred years as a sheep.
Italian Proverb

Never despair.
But if you do, work in despair.
Edmund Burke

Success is going from failure to failure
without loss of enthusiasm.
Winston Churchill

There are no secrets to success.
It is the result of preparation,
hard work, and learning from failure.
Colin Powell

Failure is, in a sense, the highway to success,
inasmuch as every discovery of what is false
leads us to seek earnestly after what is true.
John Keats

The harder the conflict, the more glorious the triumph.
We obtain too cheaply, we esteem too lightly;
'tis dearness only that gives everything its value.
Thomas Paine

The difficulties and struggles of today
are but the price we must pay for
the accomplishments and victories of tomorrow.
J. H. Boetcker

Many of life's failures are people
who did not realize how close they were
to success when they gave up.
Thomas Edison

There is no failure except in no longer trying.
There is no defeat except from within,
no real insurmountable barrier save our own
inherent weakness of purpose.
Elbert Hubbard

Failure is often the line of least persistence.
Source Unknown

You never really lose until you quit trying.
Mike Ditka

It's always too soon to quit.
Zig Ziglar

Always do more than is required of you.
George S. Patton

If you continue toward your goal,
it will happen but not necessarily
on your time schedule.
Ken Blanchard

Nothing is so fatiguing as the
hanging on of an uncompleted task.
Henry James

Consider the postage stamp, my son.
It secures success through its ability to
stick to one thing till it gets there.
Josh Billings

Winners are those people who make a habit
of doing the things losers are uncomfortable doing.
Ed Foreman

Character is the ability to carry out a good resolution
long after the excitement of the moment has passed.
Cavett Robert

That which we persist in doing
becomes easier for us to do.
Not that the nature of the thing itself
has changed but our power to do it is increased.
Ralph Waldo Emerson

The secret of success is constancy of purpose.
Benjamin Disraeli

Only one who devotes himself
to a cause with his whole strength and soul
can be a true master.
For this reason mastery demands
all of a person.
Albert Einstein

From my point of view,
it is immoral for a being
not to make the most intense effort
every instant of his life.
Jose Ortega y Gasset

I can not imagine a person becoming a success
who doesn't give this game of life
everything he has.
Walter Cronkite

If most people knew
how hard I have worked to gain my mastery,
it would not seem wonderful at all.
Michelangelo

Great works are performed,
not by strength, but by perseverance.
Samuel Johnson

Genius is only the power
of making continuous efforts…
How many a man has thrown up his hands
at a time when a little more effort,
a little more patience,
would have achieved success.
Elbert Hubbard

Genius is one percent inspiration
and ninety-nine percent perspiration.
Thomas Edison

Far and away the best prize
that life offers is the chance
to work hard at work worth doing.
Theodore Roosevelt

A total commitment is paramount
to reaching the ultimate in performance.
Tom Flores

Effort is the measure of a man.
William James

By the work one knows the workman.
Jean de la Fontaine

Excellence is not easy.
Richard Bach

The quality of a person's life
is in direct proportion
to their commitment to excellence,
regardless of their chosen field of endeavor.
Vincent Lombardi

It's a funny thing about life;
if you refuse to accept anything but the best,
you very often get it.
W. Somerset Maugham

Life is not always a matter of holding good cards,
but sometimes, of playing a poor hand well.
Robert Louis Stevenson

Such is life,
falling over seven times
and getting up eight.
Roland Barthes

Our greatest glory consists not in never falling
but in rising every time we fall.
Ralph Waldo Emerson

Big shots are only little shots
who keep shooting.
Christopher Morley

The person who makes a success of living
is the one who sees his goal steadily
and aims for it unswervingly.
That is dedication.
Cecil B. DeMille

He turns not back who is bound to a star.
Leonardo da Vinci

We will either find a way,
or make one.
Hannibal

The only way out is through.
Robert Frost

It is always your next move.
Napoleon Hill

Phase
Nine

Evaluating
Efforts

X   I
II
VIII   III
VII   IV
VI   V

Evaluating Efforts

This phase is about exploring where you are, what you've learned, and what you need to do to complete your goals. You're in a new place from where you started on this journey. It's important to learn everything you can from your experience so that you can build habits of effectiveness that can help you achieve any goal you desire.

One way to evaluate your efforts is to reflect on the following questions:

- What have you done up to this point? What worked and what didn't? What knowledge, skills, or attitudes made the biggest difference in your results?

- What important lessons do you want to remember to repeat, or be sure not to repeat, the next time?

- What do you need to do from this point forward to get back on track or bring your goals to successful completion?

A word about disappointing results. If your efforts didn't produce all that you expected, don't think of it as failure. View it as feedback directing you to apply a new approach. Learn to convert mistakes, setbacks, and failures into valuable experiences that teach you what to do—or not do—the next time around. This ability will turn any failure into success!

Also, when evaluating efforts, look for progress and not for perfection. The "curse of perfectionism" can contaminate any outcome and discourage learning. Take pride in your successes and focus on what you did well. Learn from your mistakes, resolve to do things better in the future, and give yourself permission to be less than perfect. Doing this will teach you important lessons about forgiveness, compassion, and success. You'll not only achieve more, you'll become a better person in the process.

The quotes in this phase explore:

- Experience is your ultimate teacher.

- You are only in competition with the person you can become.

- Hold yourself to a standard of excellence.

Evaluating Efforts

A moment's insight is sometimes
worth a life's experience.
Oliver Wendell Holmes

Experience seems to be like
the shining of a bright lantern.
It suddenly makes clear in the mind
what was already there,
perhaps, but dimly.
Walter de la Mare

Everything that happens to you is your teacher.
The secret is to learn to sit at the feet
of your own life and be taught by it.
Polly B. Berends

Those who fail to learn from the past
are doomed to repeat it.
George Santayana

Experience is a hard teacher
because she gives the test first,
the lesson after.
Vernon Sanders Law

Practical wisdom is only to be learned
in the school of experience.
Samuel Smiles

Wisdom consists of three things:
success, failure, and an awareness
of the lessons learned from each.
Robert L. Jolles

There's only one thing more painful
than learning from experience,
and that is not learning from experience.
Archibald MacLeish

A wise man can learn
from another man's experience.
A fool cannot learn
even from his own.
Will Durant

It is no profit to have learned well,
if you neglect to do well.
Publilius Syrus

Experience is what you get
when you don't get what you want.
Tom Bosch

Experience is not what happens to a man.
It is what a man does with what happens to him.
Aldous Huxley

Things turn out best for the people
who make the best of the way things turn out.
John Wooden

Happiness lies in the joy of achievement
and the thrill of creative effort.
Franklin D. Roosevelt

We must never try to escape
the obligation of living at our best.
Janet Erskine Stuart

I have done my best.
That is about all the philosophy
of living that one needs.
Lin Yutang

When a thing is thoroughly well done
it often has the air of being a miracle.
Arnold Bennett

The reward of a thing well done
is to have done it.
Ralph Waldo Emerson

To have striven, to have made the effort,
to have been true to certain ideals—
this alone is worth the struggle.
Sir William Osler

Success lies in doing not
what others consider to be great,
but what you consider to be right.
John Gray

What is really important is not so much
what work a person does,
but what he perceives he is doing it for.
Willis Harman

The good life is a process, not a state of being.
It is a direction, not a destination.
Carl Rogers

Life can only be understood backwards;
but it must be lived forwards.
Soren Kierkegaard

Life is ten percent what you make it,
and ninety percent how you take it.
Irving Berlin

It's what you learn
after you know it all that counts.
John Wooden

A life spent in making mistakes
is not only more honorable
but more useful than a life
spent in doing nothing.
George Bernard Shaw

If I had my life to live again,
I'd make the same mistakes, only sooner.
Tallulah Bankhead

In the end, the only people who fail
are those who do not try.
David Viscott

The men who try to do something and fail
are infinitely better than those
who try to do nothing and succeed.
Lloyd Jones

Only those who dare to fail greatly
can ever achieve greatly.
Robert F. Kennedy

I'd rather be a failure at something I enjoy
than a success at something I hate.
George Burns

Success goes to your head,
failure to your heart.
Laurence J. Peter

Success isn't permanent
and failure isn't fatal.
Mike Ditka

In nature there is neither
rewards nor punishments—
there are only consequences.
Robert G. Ingersoll

There is no meaning to life
except the meaning man gives his life
by the unfolding of his powers.
Erich Fromm

To exist is to change,
to change is to mature,
to mature is to go on creating yourself endlessly.
Henri Bergson

Do not wish to be anything but what you are,
and try to be that perfectly.
Saint Francis de Sales

Don't measure yourself
by what you have accomplished,
but by what you should have
accomplished with your ability.
John Wooden

The only honest measure of your success
is what you are doing
compared to your true potential.
Paul J. Meyer

You preach a better sermon
with your life than with your words.
Oliver Cromwell

It is no use walking anywhere to preach,
unless the walking is the preaching.
Saint Francis of Assisi

We judge ourselves by what we feel capable of doing,
while others judge us by what we have already done.
Henry Wadsworth Longfellow

What we have done is the only mirror
by which we can see what we are.
Thomas Carlyle

It is not the going out of port but the coming in
that determines the success of the voyage.
Henry Ward Beecher

Phase Ten

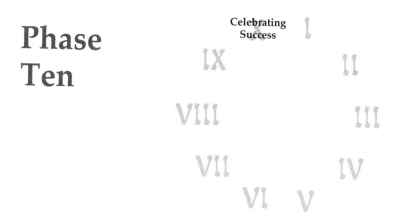

Celebrating Success

It's time to reward yourself for a job well done. There's a saying that success is its own reward, and that's certainly true with goals. But it's also important to mark the achievement of a challenging goal with something more tangible than just warm feelings.

Decide how you want to celebrate. Make your reward proportional to the achievement. There'll be bigger goals in the future and, no doubt, bigger celebrations. But, regardless of the size of the goal, something special is in order. You accomplished what you set out to do, and you deserve to mark the occasion.

Gather together the people who helped and supported you throughout your journey and celebrate with them. Although this may be your success, you couldn't have done it without their help. Let them know how much you appreciate all they did and give them an opportunity to share your joy.

153

It's important to be aware that sometimes when people achieve big goals, they feel disappointed, let-down, and adrift after working so long and hard on such a focused project. This is normal and easy to remedy. Prepare for this possibility by setting a new goal before you celebrate your current success. Make your next goal more challenging, more interesting, more motivating. Use your current exhilaration as a springboard to a new level of confidence. You did it. You can do it again, even better.

Don't forget to make a record of all your goal successes. It will help you see just how much you've done and motivate you to attempt even more. It's true that the harder the goal, the more value there is in its achievement.

Finally, remember that success really is in the pursuit of the goal, not in the destination. It's a by-product of working hard at something you deeply care about. Sure, it feels great to reach the summit, but 99 percent of the time you're climbing, so it's best to stop frequently and enjoy the view right in front of you. That's where life is savored—in the present moment. And then, with eyes wide open to exciting possibilities just ahead, keep moving toward your dreams. Congratulations!

The quotes in this phase explore:

- Success is living the kind of life you want to live.

- Success is serving others in large and small ways.

- Success is using each achievement as a springboard to a greater one.

Celebrating Success

Success is the progressive realization
of a worthy ideal or goal.
Earl Nightingale

Success is the maximum utilization
of the ability that you have.
Zig Ziglar

Success is the certain knowledge
you have become yourself,
the person you were meant to be from all time.
George Sheehan

The virtue of all achievement
is victory over oneself.
Those who know this victory
can never know defeat.
A. J. Cronin

We are the hero of our own story.
Mary McCarthy

Success is the active process
of making your dreams real
and inspiring others to dream.
James Anders Honeycutt

There is only one success—
to be able to spend your life in your own way.
Christopher Morley

A man is a success if he gets up in the morning
and goes to bed at night and in between
does what he wants to do.
Bob Dylan

The ultimate of being successful
is the luxury of giving yourself
the time to do what you want to do.
Leontyne Price

Success follows doing what you want to do.
There is no other way to be successful.
Malcolm S. Forbes

Happiness is mostly a by-product
of doing what makes us feel fulfilled.
Benjamin Spock

You never achieve real success unless
you like what you are doing.
Dale Carnegie

If you do what you like,
you never really work.
Your work is your play.
Hans Selye

The secret of success is
making your vocation your vacation.
Mark Twain

You should have a career that you love.
A career that you would want to continue
even if you were not getting paid.
To have otherwise is to cheat yourself
out of forty hours a week
for the rest of your life.
John F. Kennedy

If you are doing something you would do for nothing,
then you are on your way to salvation.
And if you could drop it in a minute
and forget the outcome,
you are even further along.
And if, while you are doing it,
you are transported to another existence,
there is no need for you to worry about the future.
George Sheehan

Life is to be lived.
If you have to support yourself,
you had bloody well better find
a way that is going to be interesting.
Katherine Hepburn

Blessed is he who has found his work;
let him ask no other blessedness.
Thomas Carlyle

There are two things to aim at in life:
first, to get what you want;
and, after that, to enjoy it.
Only the wisest of mankind achieve the second.
Logan Pearsall Smith

Happiness is not pleasure.
Happiness is victory.
Zig Ziglar

Happiness comes only when
we push our brains and hearts
to the farthest reaches of which we are capable.
Leo Rosten

I believe the true road to preeminent success
in any line is to make yourself master of that line.
Andrew Carnegie

Successful people are simply willing to pay the price
and do the things that are necessary
in order to achieve their dreams and their goals.
Lewis Timberlake

You nourish your soul by fulfilling your destiny.
Harold Kushner

The purpose of life is to live a life of purpose.
Robert Byrne

The purpose of life is not to be happy —
but to matter, to be productive,
to be useful, to have it make some difference
that you have lived at all.
Leo Rosten

Try not to become a man of success
but rather try to become a man of value.
Albert Einstein

The highest reward for man's toil
is not what he gets for it,
but what he becomes by it.
John Ruskin

Most people think in terms of getting;
success, however, begins in terms of giving.
Henry Ford

We make a living by what we get.
We make a life by what we give.
Winston Churchill

Success in life has nothing to do
with what you gain in life or accomplish for yourself.
It's what you do for others.
Danny Thomas

What do we live for,
if it is not to make life less difficult for each other.
George Sand

One of the deep secrets of life
is that all that is really worth doing
is what we do for others.
Lewis Carroll

He who does good to another does good to himself.
Lucius Seneca

There never was a person
who did anything worth doing
that did not receive more than he gave.
Henry Ward Beecher

We are here to add what we can to life,
not to get what we can from it.
Sir William Osler

I have learned that the surest way
to make my own dreams come true
is to help others achieve theirs.
Elizabeth Engstrom

In helping others to succeed,
We ensure our own success.
William Feather

It is one of the most beautiful compensations
of this life that no man
can sincerely try to help another
without helping himself.
Ralph Waldo Emerson

You can get everything in life you want
if you will just help enough other people
get what they want.
Zig Ziglar

Your reward in life is always
in direct proportion to your contribution.
Source Unknown

The man who lives for himself
is a failure;
the man who lives for others
has achieved true success.
Norman Vincent Peale

The best portion of a good man's life—
his little nameless, unremembered
acts of kindness and love.
William Wordsworth

Give of your hands to serve and your hearts to love.
Mother Teresa

The fragrance always remains
in the hand that gives the rose.
Mohandas K. Gandhi

The best and most beautiful things in this world
cannot be seen or even touched.
They must be felt with the heart.
Helen Keller

I shall pass through this world but once.
Any good, therefore, that I can do
or any kindness I can show to any human being,
let me do it now…
for I shall not pass this way again.
Etienne de Grellet

I feel the greatest reward for doing
is the opportunity to do more.
Jonas Salk

It is high time the ideal of success
should be replaced with the ideal of service.
Albert Einstein

Service is the rent we pay for our room on earth.
Lord Halifax

Everybody can be great because everybody can serve.
Martin Luther King, Jr.

The price of greatness is responsibility.
Winston Churchill

I don't know what your destiny will be
but the one thing I do know;
the only ones among you who will be truly happy
will be those who have sought and found how to serve.
Albert Schweitzer

Life is ours to be spent, not to be saved.
D. H. Lawrence

There is no wealth but life.
John Ruskin

When you have learned how to live,
life itself is the reward.
Harold Kushner

The privilege of a lifetime is being who you are.
Joseph Campbell

To be what we are,
and to become what we are capable of becoming
is the only end in life.
Baruch Spinoza

Your sole contribution to the sum of things is yourself.
Frank Crane

Success rests with having the courage
and endurance and, above all,
the will to become the person you are,
however peculiar that may be.
Then you will be able to say,
'I have found my hero and he is me.'
George Sheehan

If you ask me what I have come to do in this world,
I who am an artist, I will reply;
I am here to live my life out loud.
Emile Zola

I am an artist at living—
my work of art is my life.
D. T. Suzuki

He has achieved success who has lived well,
laughed often, and loved much.
Bessie Stanley

Most of us would like to end our lives
feeling both that we had a good time
and that we left the world
a little better than we found it.
Phillip Slater

The greatest use of life is to spend it
for something that will outlast it.
William James

This is the true joy in life,
the being used for a purpose
recognized by yourself as a mighty one;
the being thoroughly worn out
before you are thrown on the scrap heap;
the being a force of nature
instead of a feverish selfish
little clod of ailments and grievances
complaining that the world will not devote itself
to making you happy.
George Bernard Shaw

There is only two ways to live your life.
One is as though nothing is a miracle.
The other is as though everything is a miracle.
Albert Einstein

Really great men have a curious feeling
that the greatness is not in them,
but through them.
Therefore, they are humble.
John Ruskin

We are not human beings having a spiritual experience.
We are spiritual beings having a human experience.
Pierre Teilhard de Chardin

Success is a journey, not a destination.
Ben Sweetland

It is good to have an end to journey toward;
but it is the journey that matters in the end.
Ursula K. LeGuin

The journey is the reward.
Taoist Proverb

To be successful is to achieve an objective,
but to be a success is always to have
yet another objective in mind.
Source Unknown

Each success only buys an admission ticket
to a more difficult problem.
Henry Kissinger

Life is not a problem to be solved,
but a mystery to be lived.
Thomas Merton

Out of every fruition of success, no matter what,
comes forth something to make a new effort necessary.
Walt Whitman

The way to enjoy life best is to wrap up one goal
and start right away on the next one.
Don't linger too long at the table of success.
The only way to enjoy another meal is to get hungry.
Jim Rohn

What we call results are beginnings.
Ralph Waldo Emerson

Success is never final.
Winston Churchill

There is always room at the top.
Daniel Webster

May you live all the days of your life.
Jonathan Swift

Part Three

Celebrating Success · X

Cultivating Dreams · I

Evaluating Efforts · XI

Setting Goals · II

Developing Perseverance · XII

Making Plans · III

Reinforcing Accomplishments · XIII

Aligning Attitude · IV

Overcoming Obstacles · VII

Disciplining Action · V

Ten-Step Action Plan

"Nothing comes until action is taken."
Napoleon Hill

Let Part Two be a source of inspiration and enlighten-ment whenever you need it. However, beyond the wisdom and encouragement contained in the quotes, you may need a more detailed plan that shows you exactly how to turn your dreams into real-world successes.

The "Ten-Step Action Plan" provides a powerful, yet practical process for accomplishing your goals. The steps in the plan correspond to each phase in the book. If you follow each step and complete the exercises, by the last step of the action plan you will have the tools you need to reach any goal you desire.

Feel free to progress at a pace that feels right and fits your schedule, whether you do one exercise a day, one a week, or one a month. The most important thing is to maintain momentum as you move through the exer-cises so that you stay on your path to achievement.

If you're already good at goal setting, read through all the steps and pull out any tools that might help you increase your effectiveness. If you struggle at setting and reaching your goals, follow the steps as written and you will soon discover what good goal setters know: the satisfaction of achievement.

There's no secret to this process. All it takes is some time, commitment to success, and a few dreams you'd like to make real in your life. If you have those three things, let's get to work.

Preparation Step

This step is about preparing yourself for the next ten steps.

1. You'll need the following supplies to work through the exercises in this action plan:

   ■ A journal in which you will write down everything related to the development and achievement of your goals. The easiest way to do this is to get a three-ring binder.

   ■ Eight divider tabs. Label them:
   Dreams: Capture your dreams in the many areas of your life.

   Goals: Convert your dreams into specific goals.

   Plans: Translate your goals into achievable plans.

   Progress: Track your weekly and daily achievements toward your goals.

   Accomplishments: Record your goal successes.

   Inspirations: Collect your favorite quotations and inspirations.

   Lessons: Record the "words of wisdom" you learn in your continual growth and development as a "goal getter."

Appreciations: Acknowledge the people and things you are grateful for.

■ Five to ten blank pages behind each of the above tabs.

■ One pack of medium-size sticky notes.

■ One pack of 3"x5" index cards.

2. When you've collected supplies for the goals journey, it's important to ask yourself some "tell the truth" questions, especially if you've been unsuccessful in achieving goals in the past. After you get your binder or journal set up, write down your thoughts on these questions in the "Lessons" section.

■ Are you ready to make something new and different happen pertaining to your goals, or are you somehow hoping things will magically change without effort on your part?

■ What's different this time that makes you more sure of success?

■ What else has changed in your life that will positively impact your likelihood of success?

You need to be honest with yourself on these issues. In order for things to work out differently, you'll need to do things differently than you have in the past. Are you ready to make this happen?

Step One:
Cultivating Dreams

1. Read the quotes in Phase One: Cultivating Dreams. What overall message stands out that helps you see the importance of cultivating dreams? Apply what you discovered from reading the quotes to your goals and life. Record your thoughts in the "Inspirations" section of your journal.

2. Choose five individual quotes from Phase One that you find inspirational or meaningful. Write these quotes in the "Inspirations" section of your journal along with a note about what makes each one significant to you. Read them over several times today and think about how they apply to your goals and life.

3. Here is an imaginative exercise that's a powerful aid to helping identify your dreams. Choose a date five or ten years from now and imagine having a conversation with this future you. It's best to relax, close your eyes, and take a few minutes to let this fantasy take shape. Don't try to control it, just let it unfold. When you feel finished, answer the following questions about this future you in the "Dreams" section. Feel free to stretch out the fantasy to answer the questions.

   ■ Where am I living at this time?

   ■ What work am I doing?

   ■ What am I like at this time?

   ■ What life and work accomplishments am I most proud of?

- What impact does my life have on other people?

- What do I value most in life?

- What words of advice does the future me want to share with the present me to help me become the future me?

- What dreams and goals will I need to pursue to make this my future reality?

4. Here's another exercise for cultivating your dreams and harvesting all your life aspirations. Write down your answers to one or more of the following questions in the "Dreams" section:

- When you were a child, what did you dream of becoming when you grew up?

- What do you want to be, do, see, have, or experience in your lifetime?

- What would you do for a living if money was not an issue and you knew that you could not fail?

- What daydreams do you currently have that you are not working to achieve?

- What do you want your legacy to be? What do you want to be remembered for?

5. Gandhi said, "My life is my message." What does that mean to you? What message do you want your life to be? What do you need to start doing, stop doing, do more of, or do less of to make your life reflect the message you want? Put your thoughts in the "Dreams" section.

6. Dr. Maxwell Maltz and Dan Kennedy suggest in their excellent Nightingale/Conant tape program, *The New Psycho-Cybernetics,* to set "To-Be" goals, not just "To-Do" goals. The authors say that most people set "To-Get" and "To-Do" goals but rarely think about "To-Be" goals. They recommend that we ask ourselves two powerful questions:

   - What kind of a person successfully achieves the kind of goals I want?

   - How do I match up with that person?

   This exercise helps you look at the connection between your goals and your self-image. The idea is that until you develop the personal qualities needed to successfully achieve what you want, you will be working against yourself and making the goal achievement process much more difficult. Work on "inside" goals as well as "outside" goals. Record your "To-Be," "To-Do," and "To-Get" goals and your answers to these two questions in the "Dreams" section of your journal.

7. On the following page is a list of life dimensions to help you organize and categorize the kinds of dreams you have. In the "Dreams" section of your journal, create a page for each of these categories and begin writing down all of the dreams you came up with in the preceding exercises that correspond to each of the categories. Think in terms of what

you want to be, do, see, have, learn, or experience. Add any additional category pages as needed:

- Health
- Career
- Finances
- Hobbies
- Challenges
- Personality
- Possessions
- Professional Development
- Family
- Education
- Community
- Relationships
- Recreation
- Spirituality
- Self-Development
- Other

Step Two:
Setting Goals

1. Read the quotes in Phase Two: Setting Goals. What overall message stands out that helps you see the importance of setting goals? Apply what you discovered from reading the quotes to your goals and life. Record your thoughts in the "Inspirations" section of your journal.

2. Choose five individual quotes from Phase Two that you find inspirational or meaningful. Write these quotes in the "Inspirations" section of your journal along with a note about what makes each one significant to you. Read them over several times today and think about how they apply to your goals and life.

3. Let's create some order in your dreams lists from Step One's exercises by choosing which goals you want to focus on accomplishing right now and which ones you will leave for a later time. First, review your lists and put a check mark next to those goals you want to focus on accomplishing right now.

   A suggestion: choose only three to five goals to start with, taken from the different life dimension categories you listed in exercise 7 on Step One, so that you maximize the likelihood of successfully completing them and minimize the potential to overwhelm yourself with too many goals. Get some early successes with easier goals before tackling more challenging goals. With a couple of positive experiences behind you, you'll quickly learn how many you can juggle at one time.

4. Next, take each of the goals you are choosing to focus on right now and write them as goal statements, using the "S.M.A.R.T." formula discussed in the opening essay of Phase Two. Record your work in the "Goals" section of your journal.

5. After writing your "S.M.A.R.T." goal statements, create three new pages in the "Goals" section of your journal and title them:

   ■ Long Range Goals (a year or more to accomplish)

   ■ Medium Range Goals (one month to a year to accomplish)

   ■ Short Range Goals (a month or less to accomplish)

   List your chosen goals in the appropriate time frame.

   A suggestion: Start by balancing your chosen goals with one long range goal, one medium range goal, and one to three short range goals. This will help you see some quick successes and provide some short-term gratification to sustain your efforts on longer range goals.

6. On a new sheet in the "Goals" section of your journal, draw a line from top to bottom down the middle of the page. At the top of the page, write one of the goals you have chosen to focus on right now. In the left column of the page, write all the benefits or gains you anticipate getting from achieving this goal. Then, in the right column of the same page, write all the costs or losses you think you will experience from not achieving this goal. Your answers

should indicate whether you're sufficiently motivated to see this goal through to completion. If you
don't think your answers are compelling enough,
think about what you can add to your columns to
increase your desire for this goal. If you can't think
of any, consider whether you want it strongly enough
to make it a goal, and if not, choose another goal.

Step Three:
Making Plans

1. Read the quotes in Phase Three: Making Plans. What overall message stands out that helps you see the importance of making plans? Apply what you discovered from reading the quotes to your goals and life. Record your thoughts in the "Inspirations" section of your journal.

2. Choose five individual quotes from Phase Three that you find inspirational or meaningful. Write these quotes in the "Inspirations" section of your journal along with a note about what makes each one significant to you. Read them over several times today and think about how they apply to your goals and life.

3. Take each of the goals you've chosen to focus on right now and write it across the top of a new sheet of paper in the "Plans" section. Then, while focusing on one goal at a time, imagine you've successfully accomplished that goal. Ask yourself:

   ■ How did I do it?
   ■ What actions did I take to complete it?

   Then write down every action you can think of that would contribute to the completion of that goal. Don't worry about getting them in any particular order. Go for speed, quantity of ideas, and don't evaluate anything at this time. Write down whatever comes to mind, even if it's unrealistic.

The point of this exercise is to ultimately break your big goal down into smaller sub-goals and then break the sub-goals down into as many concrete activities as you can think of that would accomplish your sub-goals.

Here are three methods to help you approach this exercise:

■ Start where you are right now and list everything you can think of doing that would contribute to achieving your goal. This is the Forward Method.

■ Sometimes it helps to do this process in reverse, meaning you start from completion and work backwards, listing everything you can think of, until you get to where you are right now. This is the Reverse Method.

■ Divide your goal into its major phases or stages (like in project management) and write down all the concrete steps that are involved in completing each phase. This is the Phase Method.

Of course, you can't know all the tasks that you'll need to accomplish, and this is only meant to be a "game plan" to get you started in shortening the distance between where you are and where you want to end up. It is very important, however, that you do this exercise in considerable detail; otherwise your plans will be too general to be workable on a daily basis.

By the time you are done, you want to have all the logistics for achieving your goal, such as:

- What do I need to do?

- How will I accomplish it?

- Who will do what part of the plan (if there are others involved)?

- When will each part be due?

- What obstacles do I anticipate encountering?

- What are my plans for overcoming these obstacles?

- What additional resources do I need?

You want to get the level of detail concrete enough so that when you look at each daily activity in your plan, it seems like a manageable task (one that could be completed in 30 to 60 minutes, or in one sitting) and one you feel can be accomplished without too much difficulty. This exercise should leave you with a lot of clear actions that build a map to your goals.

4. Your next step is to select the best ideas that you came up with, and then sequence them so that you have a good idea of the order in which the actions need to be completed.

5. Finally, determine realistic time frames for each step in your plan, keeping in mind all your other time commitments. How long will each step in your plan take to complete? What activities will you do first? Which activities will you do over the next week? Month? Schedule these in your planner. Make it a priority to work on your goals every day.

Step Four:
Aligning Attitude

1. Read the quotes in Phase Four: Aligning Attitude. What overall message stands out that helps you see the importance of aligning attitude? Apply what you discovered from reading the quotes to your goals and life. Record your thoughts in the "Inspirations" section of your journal.

2. Choose five individual quotes from Phase Four that you find inspirational or meaningful. Write these quotes in the "Inspirations" section of your journal along with a note about what makes each one significant to you. Read them over several times today and think about how they apply to your goals and life.

3. This is a ten-minute visualization exercise that you can do at the beginning of every day. Take your action plan for the day and imagine yourself completing every step in exact detail. How will you do it? When will you do it? Where will you be? Who will be there with you? Maxwell Maltz, author of *Psycho-Cybernetics*, calls this "mental rehearsal," and it is a very powerful motivation strategy. Because you have already "seen" yourself succeeding in your work, it becomes much easier to make it happen in reality. Strive to finish this exercise with an unshakable belief and determination that you can do it.

4. Copy each of your selected goals onto a 3"x5" index card or sticky note and attach it to your bathroom mirror so that you see it every morning when you prepare yourself for the day. Read each one aloud and think about what you accomplished toward your goal on the previous day, and what you are going to do that day to move your goal forward to completion. Repeat the procedure at night as you prepare for bed, by reviewing what you accomplished that day and what you want to do tomorrow.

5. Another helpful technique is to look through magazines to find pictures that literally or symbolically represent your goal. Cut them out and put them in a conspicuous place as a constant reminder of your objective. Also, you can paste the pictures on pages in the "Dreams" section of your journal and make it a habit to glance at them as you plan your week and day.

6. Write some affirmations about your goals. Affirmations are simple statements about what you're trying to achieve. When you create them, make sure they're positive, in the present tense, and stated as if what you want is already accomplished. An example of a goal affirmation is "I achieve the goals I set for myself." Write your affirmations in the "Inspirations" section of your journal and copy them on a 3"x5" index card. Carry it with you throughout the day. Read your affirmations and say them aloud several times a day until your goals are achieved.

7. Listen to motivational and inspirational audiotapes or CDs every chance you get, especially while driving in your car.

8. Read educational material or inspirational literature for 20 minutes every morning to start your day on a high note. Ask yourself: What else can I do every morning to get off to a great start?

9. Role modeling is one more effective strategy for aligning attitude. The way to do this is to find one or more people who have already achieved a goal similar to yours. Find out exactly the steps they took to accomplish it, and then do what they did. This will help you acquire many success skills and save you from making many mistakes.

   You don't have to reinvent the wheel when there are many people before you who have accomplished similar goals and are willing to share their lessons with you. Your role models don't have to be people you know nor do they even have to be alive. You can choose famous people from history to study. Ask friends and colleagues for suggestions or do some research over the Internet. Put any role modeling notes in the "Appreciations" section of your journal.

Step Five:
Disciplining Action

1. Read the quotes in Phase Five: Disciplining Action. What overall message stands out that helps you see the importance of disciplining action? Apply what you discovered from reading the quotes to your goals and life. Record your thoughts in the "Inspirations" section of your journal.

2. Choose five individual quotes from Phase Five that you find inspirational or meaningful. Write these quotes in the "Inspirations" section of your journal along with a note about what makes each one significant to you. Read them over several times today and think about how they apply to your goals and life.

3. The key to disciplining action is to form habits of success. By the end of Step Three you had broken down your goals into detailed, sequential steps with timelines for completion. Now, you need to convert those plans into actions and, if you haven't done so already, schedule the first steps of your plan onto your calendar.

It's critical that you do something immediately to begin making progress. Write those first prioritized steps as "to-do's" or appointments with yourself, and make sure they're prominently displayed on whatever planning system you use so that you can't possibly overlook them. Continually separate what's truly important from what's merely urgent. Your goals are certainly important but they are probably not urgent, or you would already be doing them.

At the end of each day, assess what you accomplished compared to what you set out to do. Enjoy the satisfaction of checking each item off as completed. Get in the habit of planning the following day as the last thing you do before leaving work, which is more effective for most people than planning first thing in the morning.

4. At the beginning of each week, review your goals, plans and action steps and identify the five most important things you want to get done that week. Another way to do this is to identify the single most important result to be accomplished in each of your chosen goals. So, if you are working on four goals, you would identify four critical results for that week, one for each goal. After you identify the results, determine the actions needed to achieve those results and schedule them on your calendar for a time when you think you'll be able to complete them. Record these critical actions and your weekly and daily progress in the "Progress" section of your binder.

5. A strategy used by many great goal achievers is to identify one thing every day that you need to accomplish but don't want to do or are resisting for one reason or another. Schedule that item as number one on your "to-do" list and get it done first thing in the morning. You will experience power and freedom from knowing that you are in control of your actions and that your commitment to your success is stronger than your likes and dislikes, moods and whims. Remember: Success requires discipline.

Step Six:
Overcoming Obstacles

1. Read the quotes in Phase Six: Overcoming Obstacles. What overall message stands out that helps you see the importance of overcoming obstacles? Apply what you discovered from reading the quotes to your goals and life. Record your thoughts in the "Inspirations" section of your journal.

2. Choose five individual quotes from Phase Six that you find inspirational or meaningful. Write these quotes in the "Inspirations" section of your journal along with a note about what makes each one significant to you. Read them over several times today and think about how they apply to your goals and life.

3. Let's get some life perspective on obstacles. What obstacles in your life were your greatest teachers? How did you handle them? How were the situations resolved? What lessons did you learn from dealing with, and overcoming, the obstacles you faced that can help you with your present goals? Make your notes in the "Lessons" section.

4. In the "Lessons" section, write the word "Obstacles" at the top of a clean sheet of paper. Draw a vertical line down the middle of the page so that you have two columns. Head the left column "External" and the right column "Internal." Then list in the appropriate column all the external and internal obstacles that you experience (or anticipate experiencing) in striving for your goals.

After you complete that exercise, take out two new sheets of paper and title one sheet "External Obstacles" and the other "Internal Obstacles." Again, draw vertical lines down the middle of both sheets so that you have two columns. In the left-hand column on the sheet titled "External Obstacles," list the external obstacles that you identified in the last exercise. Leave some space between each obstacle. In the right-hand column, across from each obstacle, write down what you can do to neutralize it or transform it from an obstacle to something that can teach you lessons about creativity, flexibility, and perseverance? When you're done, complete the "Internal Obstacles" sheet in the same way.

5. On those occasions when you hit a snag and feel stuck, identify the obstacle, look to your past experience, and see if what you are stuck on is similar to something you have encountered in the past. If it is, think about how you resolved that problem, and whether there is a lesson for you in that situation that can help you in your present obstacle? Journal your ideas in the "Lessons" section.

6. Similar to the role-modeling exercise in "Aligning Attitude," when you experience obstacles, seek out people for strategic assistance and emotional support. When you're facing difficulties you will need both kinds of help. Talk to friends who are positive, support you in your goals, and can suggest some fresh strategies to get you unstuck. Make sure you note their help and support in the "Appreciations" section of your journal.

As in Step Four, identify those people who have succeeded at what you are attempting to do and make them your mentors. Learn from their successes, and especially from their mistakes. If you don't personally know anyone who qualifies, ask friends and colleagues for suggestions. Do some research on past and present "giants" in your goal area. Learn how they overcame their obstacles and setbacks, and apply their wisdom to your situation. Nobody says you have to get there on your own. Use all the help you can get!

Step Seven:
Reinforcing Accomplishments

1. Read the quotes in Phase Seven: Reinforcing Accomplishments. What overall message stands out that helps you see the importance of reinforcing accomplishments? Apply what you discovered from reading the quotes to your goals and life. Record your thoughts in the "Inspirations" section of your journal.

2. Choose five individual quotes from Phase Seven that you find inspirational or meaningful. Write these quotes in the "Inspirations" section of your journal along with a note about what makes each one significant to you. Read them over several times today and think about how they apply to your goals and life.

3. Get in the daily habit of asking yourself three questions:

   ■ What did I do today to move toward my goals?

   ■ What do I want to do tomorrow to move toward my goals?

   ■ How do I feel about my progress so far?

   After you answer these questions, acknowledge all your efforts and your ongoing commitment to reaching your goals. If you aren't satisfied with what you're doing, resist the tendency to criticize yourself and instead refocus on your goals. Nothing is learned or gained by beating yourself up. A better strategy is to break your journey into smaller steps that you have a better chance of completing.

4. Every week, take each of your selected goals and evaluate your progress according to the plans and timelines you created. Rate yourself "excellent," "good," "fair," and "poor" and record it in the "Progress" section of your journal.

If you rate your performance poor or fair, explore whether the goal is still important to you and, if it is, think about why you are not achieving your plans. Then, think about what you can do to get back on track. If things have changed and the goal is no longer a priority to you, substitute another goal for which you have more energy and enthusiasm.

Sometimes the reason you aren't making progress on your goal is because things come up at work or at home to prevent you from staying on course. Make that okay. Most of all, don't abandon your goal just because things haven't worked out as planned. Goal setting is a tool to help you succeed, not to make you feel guilty.

If you scored yourself good or excellent, it is time to reinforce your accomplishments. For your performance, identify an appropriate reward. It should be fitting for what you have achieved and motivating enough to keep you moving toward your ultimate destination. Don't always reinforce yourself in the same way. Be creative. Some suggestions for rewards are inspirational books, beautiful pictures, motivational audiotapes, and CDs. Meals with friends give you an opportunity to share your success and receive their congratulations and support. Most important is the personal satisfaction of knowing you are well on your way to accomplishing an important goal.

Step Eight:
Developing Perseverance

1. Read the quotes in Phase Eight: Developing Perseverance. What overall message stands out that helps you see the importance of developing perseverance? Apply what you discovered from reading the quotes to your goals and life. Record your thoughts in the "Inspirations" section of your journal.

2. Choose five individual quotes from Phase Eight that you find inspirational or meaningful. Write these quotes in the "Inspirations" section of your journal along with a note about what makes each one significant to you. Read them over several times today and think about how they apply to your goals and life.

3. To be successful and to develop perseverance you must follow through on your goals, even when they are no longer novel, easy, or fun. Pay attention to any excuses you may begin telling yourself or actions that might indicate you are slipping in your commitment. This is a critical point and you need to be prepared and vigilant not to give up on your goals and yourself. Identify any counterproductive ways of thinking and behaving and work to replace them with thoughts and actions that are in your best interest. Jot down your observations for all exercises in this step in the "Lessons" section.

4. Study the lives of great and famous people who have persevered (sometimes against impossible odds) to achieve tremendous success. Follow their

examples. You could choose to explore the lives of almost anyone whose name you recognize in this book and find a compelling story to inspire you. Invariably, on their journey to success they had to endure hardships and setbacks that tested their commitment and led to a decision to persevere. Pick out one person who interests you from the index and do a quick biographical search over the Internet and learn about his or her life. Write down any lessons that help you with your goals in the "Lessons" section of your notebook.

5. Another technique to help you develop perseverance is to gather supportive people around you who willingly offer their energy, enthusiasm, and advice. Receiving your "cheerleaders'" encouragement can stimulate your natural desire, motivation and momentum. Weekly or monthly phone calls, coffee, lunch, or dinner meetings can do so much to help you remain steady over the long haul. Set aside some time this week for such calls and/or meetings. Make note of their efforts to help you in the "Appreciations" section of your journal.

Step Nine:
Evaluating Efforts

1. Read the quotes in Phase Nine: Evaluating Efforts. What overall message stands out that helps you see the importance of evaluating efforts? Apply what you discovered from reading the quotes to your goals and life. Record your thoughts in the "Inspirations" section of your journal.

2. Choose five individual quotes from Phase Nine that you find inspirational or meaningful. Write these quotes in the "Inspirations" section of your journal along with a note about what makes each one significant to you. Read them over several times today and think about how they apply to your goals and life.

3. In the "Accomplishments" section of you journal, create a new page for each life dimension category (Health, Family, Work, Education, etc.) you developed in exercise 7 of Step One. When you achieve a goal from any of the categories, record your success on the appropriate "Accomplishments" page. Keep a running log of all your major victories and significant successes along with the date you completed that goal. This will organize your achievements, help you see how diverse and balanced your goals are (or aren't), and instantly tell you where you are investing your time and energy. Your "Accomplishments" section is your resume of growth and development in the important dimensions of your life.

Another purpose of your "Accomplishments" section is to give you perspective when you are feeling down or struggling with an obstacle. By glancing through a list of your accomplishments, your "greatest hits," you will recall similar times when things were difficult and how you ultimately prevailed. This can trigger memories of past strategies, or it may just lift your spirits and help you realize just how much you have achieved.

4. It's time to fill out a report card on the goal you just achieved. In the "Accomplishments" section, write "My Goals Report Card" at the top of a new sheet of paper. Take the goal you listed and assign yourself a grade according to the following scale:

> A (for Excellent Performance)
> B (for Very Good Performance)
> C (for Acceptable Performance)
> D (for Poor Performance)

After each goal, make some notes about what you did to deserve your grade and what you learned from the experience. Consider one or more of the following questions:

- What did I do well?

- What didn't I do well?

- What did I do that I want to remember to do again?

- What did I do that I want to remember to do differently next time?

- What did I learn from this goal that can help me achieve other goals?

5. Another way to evaluate your efforts is to reflect on the goal experience you just completed and ask yourself the following questions:

With my next goal:

- What do I want to do more of that contributed to my goal?

- What do I want to do less of that detracted from my goal?

- What do I want to start doing to support me with my goal?

- What do I want to stop doing that hurt me with my goal?

- What do I want to continue doing that helped me with my goal?

6. If you haven't already done so, view yourself as a student of the goal achievement process. Study different people and their approaches to goal success. When you come across a tool or technique that adds to your current knowledge and skill, write it down in the "Lessons" section and begin to use it. That way, you continue to make gradual refinements and improvements in your goal achievement skills.

Step Ten:
Celebrating Success

1. Read the quotes in Phase Ten: Celebrating Success. What overall message stands out that helps you see the importance of celebrating success? Apply what you discovered from reading the quotes to your goals and life. Record your thoughts in the "Inspirations" section of your journal.

2. Choose five individual quotes from Phase Ten that you find inspirational or meaningful. Write these quotes in the "Inspirations" section of your journal along with a note about what makes each one significant to you. Read them over several times today and think about how they apply to your goals and life.

3. It's time to celebrate your success. What kinds of celebrations mean the most to you? Generate a list of large and small ways to celebrate. Include tangible items (something physical) as well as intangible acknowledgments (a success party). Put this list in the "Accomplishments" section.

   When you achieve your goal (or a significant subgoal), pull out a celebration idea that's appropriate to your achievement. Add to this list when you hear or read of something that sounds fun.

4. Jot a note of thanks to the people you identified in the "Appreciations" section who helped and supported you in achieving your goal. Acknowledge their contribution to your success with kind words and gestures of appreciation. You couldn't have done it without them. Let them know.

5. Finally, pause a moment to fully appreciate yourself and the many large and small efforts you made that led to your goal success. Regardless of the size of the achievement, you accomplished something important and have begun establishing habits of effectiveness that can help you achieve anything you deeply desire. Celebrate the moment by writing yourself a note of acknowledgment in the "Appreciations" section of your journal.

6. You've completed all ten steps. What now?

   Go back to your "Goals" section and choose some new goals that you're ready to take on and accomplish. Make your new goals a little more challenging than your last. Balance your goal selection between personal and professional dimensions of your life.

   Also, don't forget to continue adding to your "Dreams" section as you think of new dreams that identify the things you want to be, do, see, have, or experience in your life. This will make your action plan a continually evolving road map to your present and future success.

   You now have a system and a resource for achieving and tracking any goal you sincerely desire. Remember that the more you use this system, the greater your success. Congratulations!

Instant Inspiration

A Final Word

I sincerely hope this book has helped you achieve important goals, and that you feel prepared and motivated to take on even more ambitious ones. Now you know the phases to achieving anything you want, starting with a dream and ending with success.

If you've read through the book but haven't completed the exercises, I encourage you to commit to success here and now. The time for "someday, I'll…" is past. Make your dreams reality by taking one small step, and then another, until you reach your goals. Embark on a grand journey—you'll be amazed where you end up. You can do it!

A powerful lesson I learned a long time ago is that we *over*estimate what we can achieve in the short-term, but *under*estimate what we can achieve in the long-term. By following the principles and practices outlined in this book, you can achieve more of the dreams and goals you deeply desire.

While you strive for success, it's important to keep the goal achievement process in perspective. Goals aren't an end in themselves, but merely means to an end, and that's a life filled with purpose, balance, joy, and service to others. The ability to set and achieve goals is the essential tool to take you there.

I would enjoy hearing your thoughts about *Instant Inspiration*: how you used the book, what you found most (and least) useful, any favorite quotes, lessons learned along the way, and most of all, your success in achieving goals.

I leave you with this:

> Now this is not the end.
> It is not even the beginning of the end.
> But it is, perhaps, the end of the beginning.
> *Winston Churchill*

Make your life extraordinary!

With Best Regards,
Jerry Jerome
www.jerryjerome.com

Resources

This section provides a listing of additional resources on goal achievement and personal success. After reading this book and doing the exercises, if you want more information or tools to advance your knowledge and skills, here are books, audio and videotapes, computer software programs, and websites for you to explore.

Books

Bach, Richard. *Illusions*. New York: Delacorte Press, 1977.
[Note: Richard Bach has many excellent books, including *Jonathan Livingston Seagull, The Bridge Across Forever, One,* and *There's No Such Place as Far Away.*]

Bristol, Claude M. *The Magic of Believing*. New York: Simon and Schuster, 1985.

Covey, Stephen R. *First Things First*. New York: Simon and Schuster, 1994.

_____. *The Seven Habits of Highly Effective People*. New York: Simon and Schuster, 1989.

Davidson, Jeff. *The Complete Idiot's Guide to Reaching Your Goals*. New York: Alpha Books, 1998.

Edwards, Paul and Sarah. *The Practical Dreamer's Handbook*. New York: Jeremy Tarcher/Putnam, 2000.

Ellis, Keith. *The Magic Lamp*. New York: Three Rivers Press, 1998.

Emerson, Ralph Waldo. *The Essential Writings of Ralph Waldo Emerson.*, New York: Modern Library, 2000.

Graham, Stedman. *You Can Make It Happen*. New York: Simon and Schuster, 1997.

Hill, Napoleon. *Think and Grow Rich*. Los Angeles: Renaissance Books, 1960.

Hudson, Frederic M. and Pamela D. McLean. *LifeLaunch*. Santa Barbara, CA: The Hudson Institute Press, 1996.

Leider, Richard J. *The Power of Purpose*. San Francisco: Berrett-Koehler, 1997.

Levinson, Steve and Pete C. Greider. *Following Through*. New York: Kensington Books, 1998.

Maltz, Maxwell. *Psycho-Cybernetics*. Englewood Cliffs, NJ: Prentice-Hall, 1960.

McNally, David. *The Eagle's Secret*. New York: Dell Publishing, 1998.

Peale, Norman Vincent. *The Power of Positive Thinking*. New York: Random House, 1996.

Rohn, Jim. *Leading an Inspired Life*. Niles, IL: Nightingale-Conant, 1997.

Schuller, Robert. *If It's Going to Be, It's Up to Me*. San Francisco: Harper San Francisco, 1998

Scott, Steven K. *Simple Steps to Impossible Dreams*. New York: Simon and Schuster, 1998.

Secunda, Al. *The 15 Second Principle*. New York: Berkley Books, 1999.

Tracy, Brian. *Focal Point*. New York: AMACOM, 2002.

Waitley, Denis. *The New Dynamics of Goal Setting*. New York: Quill, 1996.

Ziglar, Zig. *See You at the Top*. Gretna, LA: Pelican Publications, 1977.

Audiotapes

The Essence of Success—Earl Nightingale
The New Psycho-Cybernetics—Maxwell Maltz and Dan Kennedy
Courage to Live Your Dreams—Les Brown
Million Dollar Habits—Brian Tracy
Science of Personal Achievement—Napoleon Hill
Goals—Zig Ziglar
    All available through Nightingale-Conant (800) 525-9000

Videotapes

Goals: Setting and Achieving Them on Schedule—Zig Ziglar
    Nightingale/Conant (800) 525-9000
Making Your Dreams Come True—Jack Canfield
    Self-Esteem Seminars (800) 237-8336

Software

GoalPro 5.0—Success Studios Corporation (403) 256-5757 or
    www.goalpro.com
Franklin Planner Software—Franklin Covey (800) 508-1492 or
    www.franklincovey.com

Websites on Goals

www.goalsguy.com
www.goals2003.com

Miscellaneous

MotivAider®—Behavioral Dynamics, Inc. (800) 356-1506 or
    www.habitchange.com

Index

About the Author

Jerry Jerome is a trainer, consultant, coach, author and publisher. He has presented seminars and workshops to thousands of people in healthcare, education, banking, government, construction, and small business on achieving personal and professional goals and improving work performance at personal, team, leadership, and organization levels.

He is president of Jerry Jerome Productions, Inc., a corporation based in Phoenix, Arizona, which offers many professional development training programs that provide practical solutions to practical work problems. A theme that runs through all of Jerry's training programs is helping individuals and organizations re-ignite a passion for work.

Prior to starting his own company, he was director of leadership development for the largest hospital system in Arizona. He holds Masters degrees in both counseling and education, has taught at the college level, and was a therapist for 14 years.

Whether in "one-on-one" coaching sessions or in front of a large group, Jerry's practical approach and engaging style help people create new possibilities for personal, interpersonal, and career success.

If you are interested in having Jerry Jerome consult or present for your organization, please contact him at:

Jerry Jerome Productions, Inc.
PO Box 93006
Phoenix, Arizona 85070-3006
(480) 759-2987
www.jerryjerome.com

Order Form

To order additional copies of *Instant Inspiration*

Call toll-free: with MC or Visa, call 1-877-791-2987
      Hours: 8:00 a.m. – 5:00 p.m. MST (Monday-Friday)
Fax: 1-480-706-8808
      Hours: 24 hours a day/7 days a week
By Internet E-mail: www.instantwisdompublishing.com
Mail: Just fill out the information below and send with your remittance to:
      Instant Wisdom Publishing
      PO Box 93006
      Phoenix, AZ 85070-3006

Sales Tax: Please add 8.10% for books shipped to Arizona addresses.

Shipping/Handling: Book Rate is $3.00 for the first book and $1.00 for each additional book. Priority mail is $4.00 per book.

Please send me the following items:

Quantity	Title	Unit Price	Total
	Instant Inspiration	$14.95	
	Shipping and handling		
	Arizona sales tax		
	Subtotal		

Name:_____

Company Name:_____

Address:_____

City:_____State: _____Zip Code:_____

Daytime telephone:_____

E-mail address:_____

Payment: ❑ Check   ❑ Visa   ❑ MasterCard

Card Number: _____Exp. Date: ___/___/___

Name on Card: _____